D0987724

Oasis

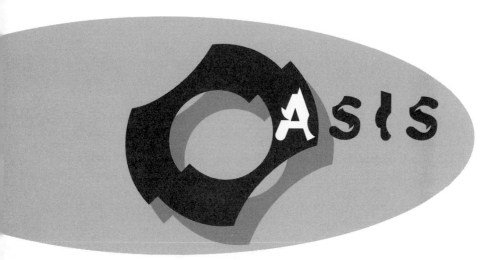

OAsis

**supersonic
supernova**

michael krugman

st. martin's griffin ⚬ new york

All photos © LONDON FEATURES International Ltd.
3 Boscobel St.
London, NW8 8PS

Design by Bryanna Millis

Library of Congress Cataloging-in-Publication Data

Krugman, Michael.
    Oasis : supersonic supernova / Michael Krugman.
      p.   cm.
    ISBN 0-312-15376-7
    1. Oasis (Musical group) 2. Rock musicians—England—Biography.
I. Title.
ML421.O27K78 1997
782.42166'092—dc21
[B]   96-37419
                                              CIP
                                              MN

First St. Martin's Griffin Edition: July 1997

10 9 8 7 6 5 4 3 2 1

For Jen Garrett
Because she *knows*. . . .

table of contents

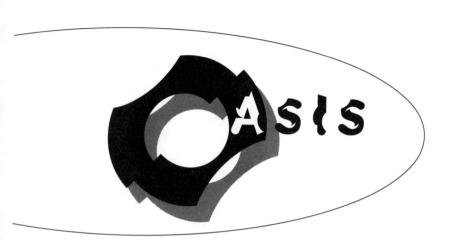

introduction

mad for it!

Sunday, August 11, 1996

For the second day in a row, 125,000 of the happiest people in England stand together on the rainswept field of Castle Knebworth quaffing pints, chanting football doggerel, poised for the singsong to end all singsongs, the biggest single-headliner gig in British history.

The weekend past, in the driving rain and cold winds of Scotland's Loch Lomond, Oasis had played two concerts to a total of 80,000 punters, but those shows were but chilly warm-ups for these. The pair of shows at Knebworth, the site of legendary performances by Led Zeppelin and the Rolling Stones back in the seventies, are the largest, most important gigs they've ever played.

That week in the U.K., it seemed as if the stroppy mugs of Oasis were everywhere. A glorious vibe about the Knebworth weekend had permeated the country, a sense of nationalistic pride and the knowledge that this was indeed going to be something special, a genuine you-shoulda-been-there event. Scalped tickets were reported to be going for upwards of $500 and the Saturday edition of the Rupert Murdoch–owned (but still staid) London *Times* even saw the boys in the band appearing in a group hug on the front page above the fold. There is no doubt about it. Oasis is, for this moment, the proverbial Only Band That Matters.

The five Manchester lads burst upon the scene in 1994 looking and acting like the Last Gang in Town, the rock 'n' roll band the world had been waiting for. From the start, it was as if Oasis had absorbed all the classic archetypes—the melodic songcraft of the Beatles, the devil-may-care attitude of the Stones, and the guttersnipe aggression of the Sex Pistols—then spat it back out, remade and remodeled for the nineties. What more could anyone want?

It appeared that they were unstoppable, these five men: drummer Alan White, bassist Paul "Guigsy" McGuigan, guitarist Paul Arthurs—better known and beloved as "Bonehead"—and of course, Liam and Noel, Ma Gallagher's thickly eyebrowed boys their ownselves. Noel, the remarkably gifted songsmith and lead guitarist, the Chief, the Leader of the Gang. At the mike is the Muscle, the Hard Guy: Liam the younger, a sneering, snarling raw nerve of a performer and the brash possessor of one of rock's most singular voices. These two very different young men, often at verbal and physical odds as only brothers can be, were supplying the bit of rough and handful of trouble that had been sorely lacking in modern pop music.

Since their beginning, Oasis have delighted in the essence of true-life rock 'n' roll adventure. Three years of swinging fists and shagging birds, fights with the audience and with each other, bad gigs and great gigs, not to mention a seemingly endless series of all-nighters fueled by lager and assorted stimulants. In their wake, Oasis left behind a trail of trashed hotel rooms, enthralled audiences and, oh yes, two timeless albums filled to the brim with Noel's seemingly inexhaustible stream of infectious, irresistible rock 'n' roll songs.

This melding of pure pop with a "come and have a go if you're hard enough" swagger confirmed Oasis as the band whose destiny was to restore classic English rock 'n' roll to the planet after years of post-Nirvana Yank grunge imperialism. Even xenophobic

America, who hadn't truly fallen for a British band in a decade, couldn't resist their inexorable force.

Amidst an overture of roaring *Apocalypse Now* helicopters and the taped caterwauling blues of "Swamp Song," Oasis takes the massive Knebworth stage to the joyous shouts of the faithful. Liam, resplendent in long hair, cool shades, and a thick wool turtleneck, circles his stage like he's ready to combust, as a giddy Noel straps on his Gibson, leans into the mike and greets the assembled.

"This is history!" . . .

one

the dreams
of children

"Somebody was playing a joke when they made me," Noel Gallagher once said. "You know, 'Let's make this guy a writer and a guitar player, but let's make him write with his left hand but play with his right, and let's have him born in the middle of May and give him a Christmas name like Noel, and let's make him a dodgy, schizophrenic, two-faced Gemini.' Cheers!"

While it's nice to attribute the creation of Noel to a higher power, it's more likely a number of earthbound elements came together to make him who he is. Born May 29, 1967, in Manchester, Noel was the second son of Thomas and Margaret Gallagher. Thomas—Tommy to the boys at the pub—was a construction worker and sometime country-music DJ, while his wife, known to her pals as Peggy, resided in the working-class Manchester suburb called Burnage with their first boy, Paul.

"Growing up was just one of them things," Noel said later. "You've got to do it, you've just got to get on with it, make the best of it."

Little Liam arrived in the Gallagher household five years later, on September 21, 1972. The brothers were forced to share a bedroom, something that always peeved Noel to no end, seeing how Paul, just a year and a half older than him, had his own room. But, Liam and Noel made the best of it, and the bedroom saw the beginnings of the somewhat loving, often heated relationship between the siblings. The boys kept a running record of their childhood by scrawling on their wall, later described by Tommy as their "wonderwall." "Bits of songs, poems, favorite bands, football teams," recalled Dad. In one corner Noel wrote 'I Love Diane Jones' and underneath, in the same writing, 'Liam is a puff.' They'd fight terribly about who had the most writing space."

In addition to the difficulty of cohabitating in such close proximity, the age differential of five years meant that the elder and junior brothers Gallagher were constantly rucking. "It's the theory of relativity, isn't it?," Noel said in *Q*. "When I was fifteen, he was ten. A social life with him was inconceivable. It's laughable to think I'd end up in a band with him. But here we are. I'm twenty-eight and he's twenty-three. Such is life. When I'm sixty-five, he'll be sixty and it'll be irrelevant, we'll both be old together."

Despite the never-ceasing bickering, Noel and Liam did find common ground. Under Tommy's tutelage, they both grew to be avid football—that is, soccer—fans, preferring the hapless Manchester City squad to the omnipotent Manchester United, the Dallas Cowboys of the British league. Their dad even formed a local under-fourteen football team.

The lads made their stage debuts in the annual school Christmas pageant. Their father remembers his youngest boy wearing a little fluffy suit in his primary-school production. "I think he was a sheep or a lamb," Tommy recollected later.

In addition to their love of footie, the lads also became enamored with rock 'n' roll. Both Noel and Liam were big fans of tubby seventies glamrocker Alvin Stardust. "When he came on telly they'd mime along and pretend to be Alvin," their father remembers, "and I'd always catch them singing into hairbrushes and playing air guitar."

"When I was a kid I thought my pop-star heroes came from

outer space," Noel laughed later in *Select*. "I didn't think they were like me. When I saw Bowie on *Top of the Pops*, I thought he came from Mars. I was disappointed when I found out he was called Jones and came from Battersea."

Most important to Noel's musical growth was the North's all-time greatest band, the Beatles. Like many youngsters, the nascent songsmith first fell in love with the Fab Four via their red and blue hits collections, and they formed the basis of his musical sensibility for years to come.

"I was about six when I started getting 'the Red Album' out," he recalled in *New Musical Express*. "They're songs to grow up with, really.... 'The Red Album' documents the Beatles as the greatest pop band ever and 'the Blue Album' documents them as the greatest rock band ever."

In most ways, Noel was a typical late-seventies preteen, enjoying sports and, like every other kid on earth at the time, a healthy fascination with *Star Wars*. "Basically, it's a love story about some guy going to rescue some bird, but the special effects were top," he gushed years later in *NME*. "I bought the dolls and the light sabers and all that shit. I paid to go see it at the cinema, and it was just complete wonderment."

He kept a sketchpad in which he chronicled his coming-of-age with poems, doodles, favorite lyrics, and lists of bands. The No Nukes movement of the period was reflected in his drawings of mushroom clouds interspersed with youthfully idealistic sloganeering like "Why must we destroy this planet?" and "This whole world is rather huppity-tuppity."

Despite his activist leanings, Noel's school life was problematic at best. While he was plainly a bright young man, he battled with a minor case of dyslexia, which, topped with the poor quality of Manchester's schools, was a dangerous combination.

"School didn't really hold anything for me," he explained later. "I knew from a very early age what I wanted to be, I wanted to be a musician. There was just nothing there for me that ever encouraged the musician in me at all. A lot of numbers, and stuff like that. As soon as I learned to read and write I didn't even bother turning up half the time. I can't add up to save me life, I can't add six and nine. I can read and write. I can't even spell, but who needs to spell?"

A chronic childhood kidney infection gave Noel his first taste of standing apart from the crowd. Because of his ailment, young Noel was not required to adhere to his primary school's dress code. "I was the only kid allowed to wear long trousers," he remembered in *Q*. "The others had these little gray shorts like something out of *Kes*, and I had these dead cool black skintight trousers with little Doc Martens. Everybody hated me."

Liam, on the other hand, was shy and almost friendless. In the neighborhood, the youngest Gallagher was known as "Peggy's shadow." "It wasn't Liam's fault," said Tommy. "All the lads round here were Noel's age and all the kids Liam's age were girls. So he'd play with the big lads, he'd come in with a bloody nose, a knock or a cut. When Peggy went out, Liam went with her to keep out of trouble."

Liam was also quite timid around the ladies according to his dad. "Up until he was fourteen, he used to say, 'I hate girls, they do my head in.' Noel was the champ with girls. He had a good few girlfriends. Diane Jones was one of the nicest, really respectable. I think she caught him with someone else, though. He used to sneak girls into the house. If I found them misbehaving in the front bedroom, I'd throw them out. Our Noel usually took girls upstairs, but only because that was where the record player was. He'd play music to them all night."

More often than not, though, Noel was engaging in the kind of juvenile delinquency that permeates working-class neighborhoods everywhere. "There were plenty of lads who were a bad influence," Tommy said later. "There was a group of lads who robbed a house and I got to know Noel was involved. He told me he was only doing lookout, but I made him tell me where the stuff was and then I took it back to the police. He didn't do it again."

"I was a bit of a rogue when I was young," Noel told *Vox*.

"I used to wag school and be into fuckin' glue-sniffing and stuff. Then me and this lad robbed our corner shop, which is a very stupid thing to do,'cos everyone knows exactly who you are. Anyway, I was put on probation and I got grounded for six months. I had absolutely nothing to do. Everyone else was going out and I couldn't be bothered doing my fuckin' homework. So I just sat there playing one string on this acoustic guitar. I thought I was really good for about a year, until someone tuned it up. Then I thought, 'I can't play the fucking thing at all now. I'm gonna have to start all over again.'"

When Noel was around thirteen, he ordered his first real guitar from the John England catalogue, "a horrible black acoustic rip-off of a Gibson Hummingbird." But from there on in, all else—school, girls, footie—took second place in his life. He practiced constantly, playing along to his favorite records over and over again. ("I can play all of *The Wall*, every single song, all the way through," he said later.)

Despite the small problem of being a left-handed guitarist with a right-handed guitar, Noel was writing songs as soon as he learned his third chord. "I was in my bedroom," he remembered later, in *Q*, of his first ditty. "Wintertime. It went G, E minor, C, D, the basic chords, right, and the chorus was, 'And life goes on, but the world will never change.' I must have been smoking too much pot at the time. It was, I dunno, just to see if I could do it. After that I wrote about seventy-five songs no one's ever heard."

Having already developed a love affair with the Beatles, the teenage Noel fell for the angry energy of punk rock. He attended his first concert in 1980, the Damned at the Manchester Apollo. While he was already musically savvy, he was "too young to be a punk, really," Noel told *NME*. "I was ten in 1977 and at that age the last thing you're going to do is listen to music. I mean, you're too busy playing fucking football or cowboys-and-Indians or something like that."

"My first memories of punk was seeing a bloke in our high street in Burnage who had big blond hair with an exclamation mark tattooed in the back of it," he recalled in *Melody Maker*. "It was like,

'Fuck! Look at that freak over there,' and he had a Sex Pistols T-shirt on, so I always associated them with freaks. When I first bought the album it was a good few years after it first came out and it frightened the life out of me. And the reason I loved it was because me mam hated it and used to tell me to take it off. I thought it must be good, then."

While he may have been too early for the first wave of punk, Noel was right on time to be taken in by the electric mod genius of the Jam, then the most popular band in the U.K. He might not have yet appreciated the brilliantly acerbic social commentary of Paul Weller's songwriting, but he was taken in by the band's unadulterated passion. "They were the first band I can recall buying," he remembered in *NME*. "When I saw Paul Weller on the TV for the first time, he's, like, chewing gum and he's got an edge and he's playing the guitar like it's going to be his last time to play it. I think that's what turned me on to them, really."

Manchester in the early eighties was, like the rest of England at the time, a hotbed of great bands. The post-punk years spawned any number of important combos, be it the gothic death-knell of Joy Division, the giddy punkpop of Buzzcocks, or, most importantly to Noel, the magnificent Smiths.

"There was a big hole in my life after the Jam split up and then came the Smiths," he said in *NME*. "They were just so different from anything else. You'd see Morrissey on *Top of the Pops* and you just went, 'What the fuck's all that about?' And you had Johnny Marr, my favorite member of the Smiths, with this big bowl haircut with sunglasses who looked like Brian Jones with black hair. And they had great songs!"

Noel saw the Smiths at Manchester's Free Trade Hall in 1984, and it had a huge impact on him. "I was a big fan and I had the records, but I didn't know much about them, really," he remembered in *Q* later. "When we got there, the whole place was covered in flowers, and I thought, 'Fucking hell, that's pretty weird.' Plus it was the first gig I'd been to where there was loads of girls and straightaway I thought, 'I like this band.' I said to all my mates, you've got to see this band, the Smiths. 'Even if you think they're shit, there's loads of fanny.' "

In April 1986, Peggy took her sons and left Tommy, and from all accounts, the split was highly acrimonious. Liam, for one, never really got over it. "I fucked him off, he's a dick," he told *Rolling Stone*. "I haven't seen him for years. He knows he fucked up. You can't patch that up, can you?"

Noel, being a few years older, was more philosophical about his parents' breakup. "I think we accepted that it was going to happen about three years before," he told *Q*'s Phil Sutcliffe, "so when it did, it was relief. I was only concerned for me mam."

Peggy supported herself and her three growing boys by working at the nearby McVittie's factory, plucking misshaped Jaffa Cakes (a ubiquitous British marmalade-filled crumbly cookie) off the production line. "She used to come home with bin-bags full of them," Noel said, "Anytime me aunties would come round, she'd be going, 'You want a biscuit?' You could see them, 'Fucking Jaffa Cakes again!' "

With their mam off working, the latchkey Gallagher boys were left on their own a great deal. Noel and Paul, already in their teens, were too busy doing their own growing up to be a surrogate dad to little Liam. "This might seem very cold and hard," Noel told *Rolling Stone*, "but when you're from Manchester, I wouldn't say it's a brutal upbringing, but it is a very down-to-earth, working-class upbringing. You've got more things to worry about than your little brother's emotional stability. You've got to make a fucking living to make ends meet."

Noel took on a series of thankless teenage jobs, including a position as a sign writer for a real-estate agent and stints in a bed factory and a bakery. As crap as those jobs might have been, nothing compared to the horror of working with Tommy on building jobs, with Liam washing the vans for some pocket coin.

"The worst thing in the world is working with your dad," Noel told *Q*. "You can't do anything right. People ask what it's like being in a band with your brother and I think, 'What about being on a building site in January when it's hailstoning with your dad and your two brothers and two of our cousins and two of your uncles and you fuckin' hate the lot of them?' Because we were always arguing we'd still be working at nine o'clock every night. Then we'd argue about whose fault it was we were late and then, when we got home, Mam'd had the dinner in the oven for hours and she'd start kicking off. Years of just rowing. We were the Clampetts, the Burnage Hillbillies."

Like so many working-class kids, Noel found solace and joy in the simple things. "When I was back from work," he said, "there was nothing else to do. Playing football, taking drugs. Football, drugs, and fucking women, I suppose, and music.... That's what life was for me."

With a lifestyle devoted to the pursuit of good times, Noel's mother had good reason to worry about her boy's future. "I left school with no qualifications whatsoever," Noel said, "and I remember me mam sitting down one night and going, 'What is going to become of you?' I didn't have an answer. But the only thing I was good at, the only thing that would make me get off my arse was that plank of wood."

He took a job with a building firm who subcontracted to British Gas. There the pivotal moment of Noel's young life occurred. While laying a huge steel gas pipe, the heavy cap dropped onto his right foot, smashing it to bits. After the injury he was given a cake job in the storehouse, dispensing nuts and bolts and the like. He soon discovered that the position meant that he would be alone for days on end and he began bringing his guitar to work with him. It was there that Noel truly tapped into his songwriting muse, composing four of the songs that would later appear on Oasis' debut album.

"People were laughing, yeah," he told MTV, "going, 'What are you doing?' 'I want to be a songwriter.' 'A songwriter? Why can't you be a drug dealer like the rest of us?' "

Meanwhile, Liam was having troubles of his own. His academic career seemed to be going along the same track as his brother before him. "I hated school," he said later. "I didn't go. Every time

I went I was in trouble, you know what I mean? I didn't learn nothin' from it, I still don't know what seven nines are."

In a way, his constant acting-out can be chalked up to the troubles at home in addition to a distinct lack of encouragement from his teachers. "I went to fuckin' school and I got some dick telling me what I was gonna do," he bitched in *Vox*. " 'You're gonna do this, you're gonna do that, you're gonna be in prison soon,' and at the time, I thought, 'You're the teacher, maybe you're right,' and I started to believe it."

After a fight that concluded with him getting conked on the noggin with a hammer, Liam was booted out of school. But seeing how he was miserable there in the first place, he quickly made the best of the situation and got a construction job building fences. "Everybody else was in school, and I was making seventy pounds a week," he remembered. "I was fucking rich. So fuck them. I told the teacher he could stick it up his ass."

At home however, the workingman couldn't get his head around Noel's increasing fascination with rock 'n' roll, a state of mind that lent itself to innumerable disagreements with the older roommate who was growing more and more devoted to his instrument. "What it was, right, I weren't into music," Liam told *Melody Maker*'s Calvin Bush. "I'd be like, 'Shut up with that bunch of crap you're playing on the guitar, you can't play it, shut up.' I was into football, and being a little scally and that."

Though his anti-music stance was most likely a form of repressed rebellion against his brother, it wasn't just Noel who served as the target of Liam's antipathy towards musicians. "Anyone that walked past me with a guitar would get loads off me," he added in *Vox*. " 'You fuckin' freak. You weirdo, playing music.' I just thought it was all weird."

The late eighties saw Manchester becoming the center of the British pop universe as the "Madchester" sound began. An intoxicating combination of Detroit house music, jangly indie rock, and pure Manc attitude, bands like the drug-crazed Happy Mondays typified the loose-groove party-lad vibe of the Manchester scene. The breakout band of the time was the Stone Roses, whose paint-splattered baggy pop would literally blow young Liam's mind. On his twenty-first birthday, Noel, now a fixture in the Manchester music world, took his little brother to see the Roses and from that night on, he would no longer have to listen to Liam's anti-music lunacy.

"Listen, this guy shared a room with me for years," Noel remembered in *Melody Maker*. "He didn't know what the fuck he was going on about, until the Stone Roses, and he could totally identify with Ian Brown. And I went, 'Now d'you know what I've been talking about for the past ten years?'"

"I can't explain it," Liam told *Vox*'s Lisa Verrico, "but when I saw the Stone Roses onstage, it did something to me. They were real people, doing it from the heart, and they just treated everything about themselves dead special."

Noel, too, claimed to have been inspired. "When I saw the Roses, I just thought I could do that."

"You would, though, you cunt," sniped Liam.

"Of course I would," his older brother said, noting, "And I did, didn't I?"

While the Madchester pop bands took the spotlight, the real scene revolved around the dance music found at the city's clubs, notably the Hacienda, which was owned by the members of local gods New Order. Though Noel had little trouble dropping E's (Ecstasy) and losing himself on the dance floor ("though I never ran around bare chested or anything like that"), the musically judgmental Liam never took to the house sound. "I think it's naff, me," he said later. "It depends on what you call dance music. Sly and the Family Stone is dance music. . . . Sly Stone is good music, right. But all this dance music these days is that same silly beat going *DANK DANK DANK* and some guy singing, 'We're all free' when you're not. It's shit. You go round someone's house and they put a tune on, and it goes *DANK DANK DANK*, and you sit there and have a cup of tea, and it's going *DANK DANK DANK*. I've got to slag it right off. It's doing my head in."

In 1988, Noel was invited to audition with a club friend's

new band, which they were calling Inspiral Carpets. "When they asked me to come and have a go, I thought, 'This is my destiny in life!'" Noel said later. "I did 'Gimme Shelter,' shouting me head off like Shaun Ryder, and they turned me down."

Nevertheless, Noel knew his guitars and the members of the organ-driven psychedelicists figured that he'd be a handy guy to have around. Inspirals capo Clint Boon reflected on the first meeting in *Vox*. "He could sing alright, but he didn't have the Inspirals groove, so we just said, 'You can be a roadie if you like.'"

"It was a great chance to suss it all out for three or four years," Noel told *Q*. "Being around managers, agents, record-company people, journalists. I'd just sit there never saying a word to anyone."

Noel finally had a job that he could really relate to, and he took to the roadie's life like a duck to water. He became so proficient that he would conduct Inspirals soundchecks single-handedly while the band partied back at the hotel. More importantly, he had the chance to figure out his own music by practicing his tunes with monitor engineer Mark Coyle on drums.

After a gig in Amsterdam, Noel and Coyle had a brief encounter with customs authorities upon returning home to Manchester Airport. The pair had taken a later flight back, and unbeknownst to them, some members of the band and crew who had arrived earlier had been busted for carrying in some smokable substance. "So they went through the list of all the people in the party," Noel laughed later, "and found out there was two left. Next day we're waltzing into the airport, stoned as a pair of runts and they said, 'Can you just come over here, please?' We didn't have anything, but they strip-searched us and all that shit, which was pretty horrible. Not quite finger-up-the-arse, just a quick look."

The best thing about Noel's career as roadie was the opportunity it gave him to suss out the music biz. He discovered that, despite the fantasy, the rock 'n' roll lifestyle wasn't just sex, drugs, and getting to the venue on time. Of course, there was plenty of sex and drugs, but still . . .

"There's nothing that's new to me in the music business any more," he explained to Lisa Verrico in *Vox*. "I've met all the record-company executives and the bullshit producers and I know that they're all assholes. I've already done all that groupie shit that the rest of them do now and believe you me, I had a fucking great time. I was as loud as Our Kid is. I did the same things he did every night. But I'm not in this band to fuck about. I'm in it for the music."

Back home in Manchester, Liam (or "Our Kid," according to Manc slang for one's brother), was putting together, of all things, a band. After all, like almost every other out-of-work music fan who ever started a rock group, there really wasn't much else to do. "On the dole, I had nothing," he told *Melody Maker*. "No motivation, nothing. I just used to watch TV and dream, just sit there thinking, 'What's the point?'"

He teamed up his old school crony Paul "Guigsy" McGuigan on bass, drummer Tony McCarroll, and on guitar, one Paul Arthurs, the oldest member, known to all as "Bonehead." "It goes back to twenty years ago," Bonehead told *Rolling Stone*'s Jason Cohen, "when I was nine years old, and we were in like primary school, we were kids, 1974. Everyone was like, it was cool to have long hair them days, wasn't it, but my parents, being good Irish Catholics, were having none of it. It was short as it can get, cut short, so all these kids with long hair were looking at me and they used to call me 'Bonehead,' because I had a short haircut. So it just stuck. No getting out of it now. Some people shout, 'Paul!' and I ignore it: 'Me?'"

Calling themselves Rain, the quartet rehearsed when they could, though they clearly lacked direction. Bonehead recalled, "We had a couple of guitars, a couple of amps, Liam could sing, y'know what I mean? We had fuck all else to do. It was either get yourself together in a band or get drunk every night. Better than hanging about the streets, y'know what I mean?"

They played a few club dates in Manchester, but they simply weren't very good. "I've been there since the first gig in 1991," brother Paul told *Select*. "It was crap! Liam's vocals had something but it just didn't click."

After a few unexciting gigs as Rain, Liam renamed his little band Oasis, after a local youth center. The newly named foursome were booked to play their first gig at the Boardwalk on August 18, 1991, going on between the Catchmen and Sweet Jesus. The crowd basically consisted of Noel and a handful of Inspirals, all temporarily home from the road.

"Noel said it was the worst gig he had seen," Bonehead recalled.

"They were just an indie band before I joined," Noel explained to *NME*'s Simon Williams. "It was alright, it just wasn't rock 'n' roll. But the bassist looked good, the drummer didn't look too bad, and Our Kid looked pretty fucking cool. At that time I was a roadie, and I thought, 'Fuck me, it's looking me in the face.' So I bowled into the practice room one day and said, 'Right, change that guitar, take them shoes off, cut your hair, I'm gonna be doing this from now on.' And they just looked at me and said, 'Oh, alright, then.'"

"We had something there, obviously, and he could see that, there was something in it," Bonehead remembered, "but we couldn't write songs. And he came in, the condition was, he writes the songs, which we were all happy to go with, because the guy sat down and played us some of the songs that he'd written years ago, man, and you knew straightaway it was a classic. You could feel it."

Finally given a chance to do something with his reams of songs, Noel played the band a handful of the tunes that he had written years back at British Gas, notably a little ditty called "Live Forever." Maybe more importantly, he offered Oasis a simple choice and once the members heard the songs, it became clear that if they threw their lot in with Noel, the guitarist could indeed make good on his promise.

"I told Our Kid the band was shit," Noel told *The Face*, "but he definitely had something as a frontman. Then I said, 'You either let me write the songs and we go for superstardom or else you stay here in Manchester for the rest of your lives like sad cunts.'"

how soon is now?

Two months and one day later, the five-man Oasis played their first gig. Arrogant from the get-go, they posted a sign at the Boardwalk entrance jokingly calling for a £40 cover charge. A few dozen punters, mostly friends, witnessed a shambolic four-song set that featured "Columbia," a Liam and Bonehead–penned ditty called "Take Me," an acoustic song creatively called "Acoustic Song," and a twenty-minute cover of a then-current house hit that no one, the band included, can recall the name of.

"We asked loads of our mates to come who didn't want to pay when they got there," Noel said later, "so there was a big scene at the door with people saying, 'I'm not fucking paying three quid to see you lot.' Of course, these are all the people now who say they supported us in the beginning."

The gig "went down like a fucking knackered lift," in Noel's words, but the band weren't fazed a bit. Hell, they thought they were brilliant, and what else mattered?

"We thought they were going to be in raptures and it ended in this bowl of silence," Noel recalled. "But from that first gig on, I don't know what came over us. We knew we were the greatest band in the world. We'd go, 'Fucking Happy Mondays, Stone Roses, they haven't got the tunes we've got.' "

The Sunday afternoon rehearsals continued apace and the band finally put together a rough demo tape. Noel sent copies to Manchester's musical tastemakers, but alas, no one took any notice.

In December, Chris Sharratt, music editor at the local-listing mag *City Life*, stumbled across a copy of the tape among the many lying around his office. His review in the Christmas double ish wasn't exactly a hearty endorsement, comparing Oasis to the Inspiral Carpets and dread Madchester chancers Northside, declaring the tape, "Interesting, but I'm not too excited."

Still on the dole, the new year found the lads plugging away at Oasis, and a frustrated Noel had begun to push harder towards getting some attention. An encounter with Tony Wilson, founder of Manchester's top indie label, Factory Records, home of favorite sons Happy Mondays and Joy Division/New Order, offered some short-lived hope.

"He went into a big speech about how the music business and the press was all overrun by Cockneys, and how baggy had been killed by them all," Noel told Radio One. "We just said, 'Right, Tone! Up the workers!' Two weeks later he rung us up and said the tape was too baggy!"

Oasis continued gigging around the North, including support slots with Revenge (New Order bassist Peter Hook's not-very-good solo project) and the Ya-Ya's. Another batch of tunes, including an early version of "Rock 'n' Roll Star," were demoed. This time, the Oasis tapes caught the ears of Caroline Elleray, manager of the dancepop collective Intastella, who tipped them to DJ Mark Riley, a onetime member of Manc art-punks the Fall, and host of BBC's *Hit the North* radio show. Oasis were granted a session, though all Elleray remembers of it is that "Liam really took the room over." Riley was cohosting the show with Peter Hook, who became the target for Liam's barbed tongue.

"Why are you wearing those fucking awful leather trousers?" Liam poked at the notoriously cranky bassist, who swore that the Gallaghers would now be persona non grata at the Hacienda.

Liam, for his part, could give a damn. "Who wants to go down there?" he snarled. "It's shit!"

"I couldn't believe it," Riley said later of the session. "I thought then that if you bottled that attitude, you'd make a million."

The next night, Oasis played the Venue in Manchester as part of In The City, the weeklong confab designed to bring the London-based industry crowd up north. Playing on a bill with Jealous, Machine Gun Feedback, and Skywalker (the obscure object of the attendant A&R folks' desire), Oasis granted the lucky attendees the glorious spectacle of a Gallagher Brothers blowout. As entertaining as the tiff may have been, no one there was sufficiently moved by the band to put their name on a contract. In retrospect, Noel has said that he felt this was the night the industry passed them by.

The business' disregard wasn't the only obstacle in Noel's path. On the eve of a U.S. tour, the Inspiral Carpets deigned to fire their entire road crew—Noel included—because of the tech squad's alleged rampant consumption of controlled substances. As if things weren't bad enough, Noel was deprived of his American holiday. Sensing that he was at a real crossroads in his life, he threw himself full-on into getting Oasis some attention, mailing copies of the demo to anyone and everyone, pumping up the rehearsal schedule to five times a week, including Saturdays.

"We used to come out of rehearsal buzzing off our heads," Tony McCarroll recalled fondly in *Vox*, "thinking what a vibe we'd had in there for the past five hours or whatever. It was brilliant. I loved it."

Taking the reins, Noel hooked up with Tony Griffiths, an old pal from the Inspirals days. Griffiths and his band, the Real People, had invested in their own eight-track studio on the Dock Road in Liverpool, and Noel had hopes to record there. Griffiths agreed, and soon discovered just how little Oasis knew about the recording process. "They were quite naive about recording," he told *Vox*, "so we'd show them how to play the songs, how to think about the structure of the songs and the dynamics. We were just helping them because that's what bands do in Liverpool. I don't think it's quite the same in Manchester, because no one had done anything for them before."

The band's final gig of 1992, on November 22 at the Boardwalk, found Oasis still third on the bill, behind the Cherries and Molly Half Head. Their set was running overlong when the Cherries, perhaps unaware of the Gallaghers' propensity for getting into scraps, pulled the plug on them. An onstage shouting match ensued, and an incensed Liam spent the remainder of the night seeking vengeance.

Noel saw the gig as the start of the band's bad rep. "We were actually trying to convince people we were great," he told *NME*'s Simon Williams, "but after the first four gigs in Manchester no one would put us on because we had this reputation for being... not lads, just difficult. We had a fight with the headlining band one night 'cos they pulled the plug on us during the last song. That's when it started, because loads of A&R men had come to see this other band have this massive scrap onstage with us. It got us a bit of a reputation."

Bad rep or otherwise, the gigs continued, with the set now including a guitar-fueled cover of Hot Chocolate's seventies funk classic "You Sexy Thing." Then destiny stepped in. One fine Manchester day, Noel bumped into a Hacienda pal that he knew only as Ian. They talked a bit, about the scene, about old friends and, of course, about Oasis. Ian suggested that Noel get him a copy of the Oasis demo tape "to play to Our Kid." They chatted on, when Noel mentioned how he'd just bought The The's *Dusk*, featuring the guitar stylings of his idol, Johnny Marr. Ian noted that Our Kid was really pleased with it.

"Hang on," Noel asked. "Who the fuck's your kid?"

As luck (fate?) would have it, Ian was the brother of none other than Johnny Marr. Noel got a copy of the demo to Ian, and soon found himself on the other end of a call from his guitar hero himself. The ex-Smith congratulated him on the quality of the songs, and the pair hit it off. As they shared their mutual obsession with vintage guitars, Noel mentioned Music Ground, a guitar shop in Doncaster that he frequented. Intrigued, Marr suggested that they drive up to to the shop. That afternoon, Noel on the dole watched Marr spend £9,000 on guitars, and more than ever, could feel the hunger for success bubbling inside.

But this was to be the day the torch was passed. Johnny gave Noel the Gibson Les Paul he played on "The Queen Is Dead," which was presented to him years back by Pete Townshend. Even more importantly, Marr hooked Noel up with Marcus Russell and Ignition Management.

The Welsh-born Russell began his career promoting punk gigs at his London college. Upon graduating, he took a teaching position in Essex. After his wife left him, Russell returned to his music-biz roots, entering the management world by repping crap eighties combo Latin Quarter. Despite some success in Germany, Latin Quarter never quite made it in the U.K., though from the experience, Russell learned that making it at home was not top priority. He mastered his trade and took on a number of clients, including the Bible and Johnny Marr.

At the behest of his top client, Russell trekked up to the Hop and Grapes in Manchester to see Oasis opening for Dodgy. "I saw them and immediately felt the Oasis effect," he said of the gig later in *Select*, "a breath of fresh air, genuine quality, energy, all the things I've been hooked on in twenty years of British rock and pop music rolled into one, which hasn't happened for many years."

A deal was soon struck. "We don't even have a contract," Noel told *The Guardian*. "Just a handshake." (Asked what he'd do if Russell screwed them, Noel was fairly relaxed. "Well I'd sue him, wouldn't I?" Though when reminded about the lack of a contract, Noel had to consider an alternative method of negotiation. "Then I'd burn his house down. And he knows I would.")

Meanwhile, some friends in the band Sister Lovers tipped Noel that Alan McGee would be attending new Creation Records' signing 18 Wheeler's May 31 gig at King Tut's Wah Wah Hut in Glasgow.

McGee was the ginger-haired patron saint of the U.K. indie scene. The founder of Glasgow's Biff Bang Pow!, McGee and BBP guitarist Dick Green started Creation Records (named after their fave sixties Brit-band, the Creation), which quickly became the focal point of the C-86 movement, the short-lived but highly influential scene where fey young men with fringe jackets and foppish haircuts hyperstrummed guitars in bands with post-psychedelic monikers like the Weather Prophets, the Jasmine Minks and the June Brides. Over time, though, McGee turned out to have some of the best ears in the biz, discovering some of the late eighties most significant artists: the Jesus and Mary Chain, My Bloody Valentine, and Primal Scream.

According to legend, Oasis and their fifteen-man entourage arrived at the Wah Wah Hut and threatened to torch the place if they weren't allowed to play. "We didn't threaten to burn the club down," Noel explained later in *Q*. "We just pointed out to the owner of the club that if he didn't let us play, there were fifteen of us and three of them. So he did a quick mathematical assumption that it was probably in his best interests to let us play."

"I'd just arrived," McGee remembered, "and I'd heard about this band and how they were going to trash the gig, and I thought, 'This sounds great,' like the Sex Pistols or something. And then, when I arrived, I saw about fifteen lads around a table, and one of them looked amazing. He had this blue-and-white Adidas top on and he looked really cool, like Paul Weller or something. He turned out to be the singer."

As McGee sat in the back of the dank club, he watched as the band took over the stage. Intrigued by their laddish looks and obvious attitude, he was immediately knocked out once they began to play their four-song set. The clincher for him was the electrifying set-closer "I Am the Walrus."

After the band finished, a blown-away McGee approached Oasis. Noel remembered in *NME*: "He says, 'Have you got a record deal?' and we said no, and he said, 'D'you fucking want one? I'm the president of Creation Records!' So I said, 'Aha! So it's your fault, then, it is, you twat!' And he says, 'What do you mean?' And I said, 'Shonen Knife is your fault! It's all down to you, son!'"

"We thought he was taking the piss," Liam later told *Melody Maker*'s Calvin Bush, "'cos he was all Armani'd up, a bit of a smoothie, like. And he said to me, right, to this day, he doesn't even know what the fuck he signed the band for. Something got him in there [tapping his heart], he got butterflies in his stomach."

Maybe it was the Jack Daniel's he'd been drinking, but McGee couldn't get the scrappy Oasis out of his head. Back in his hotel room, the boss needed to share his find with someone else at Creation, just to let them know that he may have found the next next-big-thing. "McGee phoned us up from Glasgow at about three in the morning, off his nut, saying, 'I've just seen the Sex Pistols, Abbott! This is the band who'll turn the company around,'" Creation exec Tim Abbott said. "You could have had a thousand A&R men in the place that night and only Alan would have got up there and said, 'I'll sign them!' That's why Alan is a genius."

All of a sudden, the record-company weasels who had previously ignored Oasis, regarding them as hopelessly retro and uncommercial, were forced to take Oasis seriously. After all, McGee was interested, and he seemed to know how to give the people what they want. Mother Records, the vanity label set up by the members of U2, picked up on the buzz and offered to double Creation's bid, but Noel wanted to sign to "the greatest record company in the world. Bar none."

"You know Leonard Nimoy is on Creation?" Guigsy noted in *NME*. "Well, I want Spock to be our tour manager. Could you imagine it? 'You have just thrown that table out of the window. That is highly illogical, Guigsy.'"

A week later, Oasis traveled down to Creation's London offices where they saw Abbott garbed in the hated Manchester United's jersey. They'd only agree to sign to the label if Abbott "takes that fuckin' shirt off." On their next visit two weeks later, some band and label staff members ventured out on a night-long drinking session.

Noel wanted to be sure that Creation were capable of giving Oasis the backing they needed to become the biggest band in the world, insisting that they back up their promise by adding a clause into their contract guaranteeing that he would receive a chocolate-brown Rolls-Royce when they became massive.

According to Abbott, "Noel said, 'Do you believe in it? Because you have to go all the way.' "

Needless to say, the answer was yes.

three

happy boys happy

The brand-spanking-new "Creation Recording Act" spent the summer of 1993 supporting Brit folkpopsters the Milltown Brothers and Yank alterna-icon Liz Phair around the North. With five band members, two roadies, and a whole mess of equipment stuffed into one van, things were tight, but spirits were, erm, high. Noel told *The Guardian*'s Jim Shelley that the general vibe was "like a bunch of fuckin' Vikings, invading England for the first time."

With most of their tour advance blown on liquor and drugs early on, the lads were forced to resort to lighthearted larceny for the remainder of the trip. Sneaking away from hotels and gas stations without paying, that sort of thing. Noel remembers those days as wild and exciting indeed. "Guigsy used to be completely and utterly stoned twenty-four hours a day. I don't think he spoke to me for four months. Tony was just totally befuddled by it all, and me and Our Kid were like fookin' Punch and Judy."

While things were clearly improving, not every show on the tour was a success. Some were outright disasters. "There was the famous gig at the Duchess of York in Leeds where no one turned up at all," Noel larfed to *Q*'s Tom Doyle. "Not even one person. So we've actually played to less than three men and a dog, and there's not many bands who can say that. But it was great. We did an encore and everything."

After the tour, Oasis returned to the Real People's eight-track studio in Liverpool where they completed an early version of the ecstatically baggy "Columbia," which had long been the psychedelic centerpiece of the live set. McGee brought the tape to Dave Massey at Sony America, and the exec became an instant fan. "I went completely bonkers," he recalled later. "I've never responded to anything as strongly as I responded to that."

A heavy rehearsal schedule went into effect at Room Four of the Boardwalk Rehearsal Rooms, where they went through their ten-tune set over and over and over again. The other bands working at the studio (including the New Fast Automatic Daffodils) were flummoxed by the newcomers and their retro-rock songs, finally sticking a sign on the door reading, "Get Your Own Riffs!"

After a more successful appearance at the second In The City fest at Manchester's Canal Bar on September 14, Oasis headed south for their London debut at the Powerhaus on November 3. Dave Massey was in the house and found himself utterly blown away. "I started jumping around because every song was a hit," he exclaimed later, adding, "And they had the best eyebrows I had ever seen in my life!"

The gig was the closer for Massey, who officially inked the band to Sony America. All of a sudden, Oasis were a hot commodity and they embarked on tours with the Real People, Verve, and Saint Etienne.

Their support slot with Saint Etienne at the Birmingham Institute brought them the dubious honor (and rite of passage) of their first slag in the national music press. "If Oasis didn't exist, no one would want to invent them," wrote *NME*'s Johnny Cigarettes. "Vaguely trippy guitar, almost-tunes with a vaguely Ian Brown–as–Tim Burgess slob of a frontman, singing in a vaguely tuneless half-whine, vaguely shaking a tamborine. . . . Most annoying is the fact that they're too cool to have a personality or be more surprising than the dullest retro indie fops, too well versed in old records to do anything new, and evidently have too few brains to realize that any of the above is true. Sad."

Melody Maker's Calvin Bush was far more impressed by the band's set at Glasgow's Plaza. "They are one simian-jawed, crouch-backed vocalist and four mop-top, inanimate session musicians who, it's pointed out to me, play with all the derring-do of Piltdown Man thawing out," he wrote, but was nevertheless, lovestruck. "They play eight songs, seven of which are more marvelous than Lena Olin in slinky black lingerie and a bowler hat. They are, frankly, incredible."

From the get-go, Oasis were never anyone's idea of a showy band, preferring to let the music do the talking while the fans did the frenetic leaping-about. No matter how brash and powerful the music, the men of Oasis stood about the stage, ever nonchalant, with Liam firmly behind the mike. With his hands clasped behind his back, the frontman stood almost completely motionless, his electric energy focused in his visceral, vibrant vocals.

"People go, 'Yeah, man, well you're a shit performer,'" Liam groused in *Huh*. "But I didn't join a band to be a performer, man. People'll go, 'Well, your fuckin' gig was boring.' Why? ''Cos you just fuckin' stood there.' Well. Fair enough. Did you like the music? 'Yeah.' Well. What's your fuckin' problem? We gotta put that question at 'em, see? Why are you bored as shit? ''Cause you just stood there, man.' Well. Go and see the circus, then. Go and see the guy who fuckin' spins fifty-four bottles in the air and catches them in one go. We're a great fuckin' rock 'n' roll band. It ain't a show, man. Imagine if we did jump around. We'd blow the fuckin' roof off."

"I have to stand still, and look at the fucking guitar," Noel has said, "because, regardless of what people may think, I'm not that competent a guitar player. I'm certainly not that good a guitar player to jump around onstage. Plus it's too tiring, I'm just too fucking lazy. And, at the end of the day, we've actually proved that it doesn't really matter. It's not about how high you can jump in the air."

After a December 16 gig at Liverpool's Krazyhouse, Oasis headed to the nearby Pink Museum studio for four days of recording with Noel's old Inspirals crony, Mark Coyle. While there, Noel began improvising a spiraling riff, tossing out wacky lyrics off the top of his head. Engineer Dave Scott's Rottweiler was in the studio and the aging doggy's endless flatulance led to a discussion of whether the beast had been eating Alka-Seltzer. Eight hours later, the spiraling, anthemic "Supersonic" was completed.

"The song just came out of nowhere," Noel said of the sessions, "and I knew it was a fuckin' classic as soon as we'd finished."

"I had about an hour to write lyrics for this song," he told *Melody Maker*. "So I sat down with a pen, a piece of paper, and a bottle of gin and just wrote that down. Then I read it back and thought, 'Fucking hell, I'm a weird cunt, me!' "

With "Supersonic" done, Oasis trekked down to London to record their all-important debut BBC Radio One session. The evening before, Noel had met Bobby Gillespie and Robert "Throb" Young of Primal Scream and embarked on an all-night drinking spree.

"We went back to some hotel with Bobby and Throb and they had this acoustic guitar," Noel informed *Melody Maker*. "We'd just been signed to Creation at this point and they were wary of me and they were playing all these old blues numbers that I'd never heard in my life. Then Gillespie picks up this guitar and goes, 'Play us your favorite song, then.' So I just played him 'This Guy's In Love With You' and he came up to me and shook my hand and said, 'You fucking know, don't you?' And I said, 'I do.' And he said, 'You're fucking alright, you.' And I said, 'I know.' We've been best mates ever since."

The following morning at BBC's studio, the engineer walked in and asked "Where's Noel Gallagher?" only to be told, "That's him, under the control desk." However hung, Noel was able to lead Oasis through a session that featured "Shakermaker," "Cigarettes and Alcohol," "Up In the Sky," and "Bring It On Down."

Meanwhile, Creation began distributing the demo version of "Columbia" as a white-label single, and the unprecedented happened.

"It was incredibly easy," record plugger Gary Blackburn said. "They put it on the playlist straightaway."

The new year saw Oasis picked to click in both *NME* and *Melody Maker.* "Creation's latest discoveries are what the world's been waiting for," declared the *Maker* in their "Guide to Your Stars for 1994." "Oasis plunder the vaults of golden psychedelic Britpop with shameless glee. Chart hits, teen-idol status, and cascades of fool gold will all be theirs by the year's end."

For their part, *NME* was a tad reticent, lumping Oasis with another Mane group, the Smiths-cum-U2 combo, Marion, but noting that Oasis have "a languid way of mixing Santana and Happy Mondays. Sort of."

On January 8, Oasis headed to Monnow Valley Studios in Wales to record their debut album, though things didn't exactly go off as planned. "The problems started almost from the beginning," Noel told *Melody Maker.* "It wasn't with the band, apart from our drummer, who's Ringo Starr incarnate and can't keep time to save his fuckin' life."

The crux of the difficulties was the instantly adversarial relationship between producer Dave Batchelor and the band. Batchelor, a former member of the Sensational Alex Harvey Band, was determined to fine-polish their raucous sound, while Noel knew the recordings should sound raw and bustling.

"I'd be pissed," Noel told *Mojo*, "and I'd be saying, 'Let's get a bit mad here, let's get really young and compress the shit out of this so that the speakers blow up.' He'd go, 'Nope, 'cos this is the way we done it in our day, son.' I'd say I'd want it to sound like an aeroplane taking off, and he'd say, 'Oh, you mean you want a Yamaha Backwards Fucking Flange-Loop-Snubble with a Dirk on it?' "

"It was a simple case of conflicting ideas between producer and band," Mark Coyle said later. "The band weren't blameless, mind. They were using a lot of unfamiliar gear just cause it was there. Amps, preamps, gadgets and guitars that Johnny [Marr] had lent Noel. It ended up sounding like any other indie band doing Oasis songs."

Communication between all parties dwindled, as Batchelor attempted to separate the members of Oasis, setting them each up in a different part of the studio. After a week where nothing seemed to get accomplished, they relocated to a smaller room in the studio and started from scratch.

Dave Scott watched the bad vibes between band and Batchelor come close to physical violence. "When Liam dared to suggest that what he was doing sounded crap, he freaked out. With what went down that day he was lucky not to have his nose broken by the band."

Batchelor's wrongheaded approach included slowing down the Crazy Horse–gone–punk of "Slide Away" to the point where it bore little resemblence to the version Oasis had been playing live. "His original version sounded very bombastic," Scott recalled, "very Pink Floyd, like 'Comfortably Numb.' Noel asked my opinion and I said they should play it at the speed they had when they first wrote it."

"Recording an album should never have been this difficult," Noel said later. "I was busy telling everyone it was the greatest record ever made but it was sounding like shit."

Even Marcus Russell began to get worried, later remembering in *Melody Maker* that he "listened to the mixes and it was sonically weak, like it was recorded forty thousand leagues under the sea. Dave Batchelor had neutered the band. I said to Alan McGee, 'Fuck, we've got problems.'"

After eighteen miserable days (at £800 per) in Monnow, with God only knows how many more pounds spent on booze and drugs, the only complete song recorded was "Slide Away" (played at the speed God—and Noel—intended), though a bunch of shambolic Rolling Stones covers featuring Noel on vocals also made it onto tape. Still, the time there wasn't a total loss. They shot the "Supersonic" sleeve photo in the studio and Liam found himself face-to-face with his great hero Ian Brown while walking the streets of nearby Monmouth. Brown, who was in town recording the Stone Roses' five-years-in-the-making *Second Coming*, seemed proud of his influence on Oasis, telling his starstruck acolyte that they "are on the right tracks."

Four days after vacating Monnow for London's Olympic Studios, where the label could keep closer watch on the proceedings, Batchelor was booted and replaced with the more-in-tune Mark Coyle. The month ended with a January 27 show at London's Splash Club. The buzz building around Oasis came to a head that night.

"They turned up too early and then insisted on beer being served to them at four o'clock in the afternoon," Nick Moore, the promoter who booked the gig, recalled later. "I told them to piss off! It was one of the vibiest gigs I've ever been to in my life. It was rammed."

"Oasis are vital, alive," *Melody Maker*'s Sarra Manning wrote of the show. "They're going to steal your hearts, with or without your consent."

smash it up!

Flush with their newfound power, the lads began acting-out in earnest. A February 6 gig in Gleneagles, Scotland, found them pilfering a number of golf carts from the city's famous course. But that was nothing compared the incident that would forever brand Oasis as loutish trouble boys.

The band boarded the Harwich-to-Amsterdam ferry en route to a support slot with Verve in Amsterdam. A big show, this. The European debut. Alas, it was not to be. Once aboard the boat, Oasis were first introduced to the joys of duty-free shopping. They began pounding the no-tax champagne and Jack Daniel's, soon finding themselves in a ruck with a traveling band of Chelsea Football supporters. A follow-up scuffle with the ferry's security force wound up with Liam and Guigsy handcuffed and locked in the brig. While they were cooling off in the cooler, somebody had broken into Bonehead's berth, swiping his passport and all his clothes. After pounding on the doors of the neighboring cabins in a mad hunt for the culprits, Bonehead and Tony were united with their pals in the cell.

When Noel awoke in his cabin on the morning of February 18, he was ready for a lovely day in Holland. Problem was, the rest of his band were sitting in a dockyard cell, awaiting the next ferry home. Liam and Guigsy had been officially arrested, and the fighting four were being deported. Noel alone was left to inform the venue that Oasis would not be performing that evening. An official statement released upon their return summed up the affair. "Several of the band members have never been abroad before and obviously got carried away with themselves."

"I'm aggressive, but I'm not a fucking hooligan," the ever-contradictory Liam told *The Face* later. "I'm not Evan Dando, either. All this 'I do smack, I do crack,' fucking tortured artist bit. I admit it, I love snorting, I love sex, but I'm not into smashing things up. Chairs are for sitting on in my book."

"The lads get bored, get drunk, start brawling and do the rooms," explained Noel. "I go off and write music, because nothing else matters to me. If the Devil popped up now and said, 'It's a choice. Music or relationships,' be it mother, girlfriend, even Liam, I'd sign on the dotted line."

"I feel sorry for Our Kid sometimes," Noel told *NME*. "I've got all this shit going on inside my head and I can write it down and get off on that. But he can't, so his release is to get off his head."

Following the Amsterdam debacle, Oasis headed to Sawmills Studios in Cornwall in late February to continue recording, this time with Mark Coyle as studio boss. "Talk about being isolated!" Noel said of the sessions. "Sawmills is miles from fuckin' anywhere. You had to get there by boat when the tide was in. We needed to get away from Manchester, London, or Liverpool because of the distractions. We had all the tracks done and overdubbed inside ten days, just whacked through them every day until we had the right takes."

With Coyle behind the board, the vibe was far superior to the Monnow Valley sessions. His long-standing friendship with Noel, not to mention his time spent on the road with the band, gave him the ability to do right by the Oasis sound.

"Because I was their live engineer, I knew we had to 'capture' this band rather than produce them," Coyle told *Melody Maker*. "My approach was to just set them up like they are when they rehearse or play live, where they can see each other, get that vibe going between them and power up."

"The sessions were exactly as they are as people," engineer Anjali Dutt said later in *Select*. "Incredibly funny, because they're mad. It was sort of, when it happens, it happens, and you just have to get it. They don't work or stuggle at it."

In early March, Coyle and Dutt brought the Sawmills tapes to London's Eden Studios for mixing. Despite the high quality of the basic tracks, Coyle couldn't quite nail the right mix. "Some of the vocals were a little shaky," Marcus Russell recalled in *Melody Maker*, "but I knew the performances were essentially there, they just needed sorting out. That's where Owen Morris came in."

The twenty-six-year-old freelance producer/engineer, whose previous work included knob-twiddling with Johnny Marr and Electronic, is generally credited as being the man who turned things around. His mixes of the Sawmill sessions make up the majority of *Definitely Maybe*: "Rock 'n' Roll Star," "Cigarettes & Alcohol," "Shakermaker," "Live Forever," "Up In the Sky," "Columbia," "Bring It On Down," "Sad Song," "Digsy's Diner," and a remix of Batchelor's original "Slide Away."

"I tried to record the record from the word go," Morris explained later, "but they had other ideas. They completely mucked it up. It was lacking in life. I redid a lot of singing. I wanted to make the sound as heavy as possible, as I was frustrated with machines and dance music and wanted loud guitars, and luckily enough so did they."

Morris and Noel hit it off immediately, becoming fast friends. Morris was a rare breed: a studio wizard who was loose enough to become part of the gang. "What are they like?" he once said of his subjects. "They're all cunts: Noel's a clever cunt, Liam's a cocky cunt, and the other three are just cunts."

With Morris busy in the studio, the band took off on a co-headlining tour with Whiteout. After the first gig in Bedford on March 23, members of both bands and their assorted friends played Beatles songs in the hotel halls long into the night, resulting in their getting banned from the hotel. On March 24, the tour rolled into London's 100 Club, the Oxford Street jazz spot where the Sex Pistols first caught the attention of the world. This would be the night that the momentum behind Oasis exploded, and the notion of "co-headlining" would become a thing of the past. *NME*'s Ted Kessler was definitive about the gig, writing, "Tonight Oasis assume the mantle of Best Live Band In the Country with joyous, arrogant Mancunian confidence."

The tour continued through April, gathering steam and attention for the release of "Supersonic." It was decided that Noel's newest song would serve as the perfect introduction to Oasis, and as such, it would be their debut single. With its nonsense lyrics and striking guitar hook, the song served as a virtual manifesto of the Oasis spirit: "Feelin' supersonic / Give me gin and tonic / You can have it all / But how much do you want it?"

"I met a girl and I felt really sorry for her," Noel later told *NME*, "because she came up to me and said, 'I've got "Supersonic" and I'm, er, really into your lyrics and, er, I've been through a lot as well.' And I went, 'What do you mean?' 'Supersonic' is about some fucking nine-stone geezer who got Charlie'd off his nut one night ... it's not about anything! It's just about a feeling, you just get up and play it."

Obviously that feeling was contagious. The Brit crit establishment went bonkers over "Supersonic." Keith Cameron in *NME* made it "Single of the Week," declaring the tune "a paragon of pop virtue in a debut single." The single hit shops on April 11, 1994. One week later, it entered the U.K. Top 40 at number 31.

A while back someone had noted that if it were possible to bottle the Gallagher attitude, millions could be made. Well, here it was, and with the release of the single, the genie was let loose. "It'll all be apparent when 'Supersonic' comes out," Noel had told *Melody Maker*. "Then it'll all be WAY-HAY! from there."

He had no idea.

five

eight days a week

"I knew, as soon as we had the first single out, what was gonna happen," Liam told *Melody Maker*. "Suede were the only big band in Britain at the time and although we weren't doing gigs—we were stuck in a room all day, getting better and better—I just knew that if we did a few gigs and got a bit of interest, that'd be it. It would just go fuckin' mad. And as soon as 'Supersonic' come out, it did."

While the band were rapidly becoming stars, the increasing antipathy between the Brothers Gallagher was becoming problematic. While the older/younger sibling relationship was always fraught with anger and resentment, Liam and Noel's feudin' and a-fightin' was now a public spectacle.

"We argue a lot, but people argue, y'know what I mean?" Noel told *Rolling Stone*'s Jason Cohen. "We disagree a bit more often than other people do. Journalists need things to write about, don't they? All the journalists I know, if there's any way they can get round writing about the music then they won't write about the music, because it's easier for them to write that you had red socks on, or you take drugs, or you sleep with fucking loose women and stuff like that. It's interesting for the kids to read. It's better than writing that you sit in a hotel room reading fucking poetry, y'know what I mean?"

"The fighting and the feuding worked in our favor at first as it captured the public's imagination," said Creation publicity boss Johnny Hopkins. "But the downside has been that most journalists since have tried to engineer the same situation."

Meanwhile, Owen Morris was hard at work in London's Matrix Studios putting the final polish on the album.

"There comes a point were you just have to trust people," Noel said. "We were off on tour, rehearsing, and the whole thing in the press was just going mental."

"By this time the band were that fed up they couldn't be arsed about which [track] to use," Morris recalled in *Melody Maker*, "so I acted as producer and did it myself. I just got stoned and worked on arrangements.

"The only real problems I had with the actual performances was the groove on the drums. The drumming was okay, he kind of starts then stops at the end of the song, but sometimes it lacked groove. As for Bonehead's rhythm tracks, he was brilliant on every single one! Unbelievably tight and solid to the point where you didn't have to worry about his stuff at all.

" 'Cigarettes and Alcohol' was the last mix I did. I confess, I was that drunk and stoned at the end I just put the tape on and stuck the faders up, hence all the noise."

In early May, Liam and Noel joined members of the Boo Radleys and Ride for a *NME*-organized panel discussion to mark Creation Records' tenth anniversary. Those in attendence were lucky enough to witness some of the brothers' trademark bantering and bickering. Asked the worst thing anyone's ever said about them as a band, Liam complained that "I got called a blob."

"No you didn't," interjected Noel. "It was 'slob.' "

"Oh yeah," Liam said. "That was the first thing that got me. It done me head in. 'You fuckin' slob.' "

Noel pointed out that the depiction of Liam as slob was not too far from the truth. "I live with the guy and that's what he is," he noted. "He's a fuckin' slob. Ask me mam."

After the panel, the Oasis gang wound up in the Good Mixer, the Camden pub that served as the central watering-hole for members of the Britpop community, and there Liam met Blur's Graham Coxon for the first time. Liam flung abuse at the guitarist from his least favorite band with such merciless venom that he and the rest of his party were booted out of the joint. Later that night at another club, the Camden Underground, the two parties met again and yet more invective was strewn, mostly by Liam, of course. Once again, the evening ended with the Oasis camp asked to leave the premises.

Despite the increasing viciousness of Liam's anti-Blur campaign, Blur boss Damon Albarn took the high road when he commented on Oasis in *NME*: "It's important that Oasis are rude about everybody and that they get drunk. That's what people like you want, and you encourage them. Fair enough. It's nice, isn't it? But it's nothing to do with me. They came to see us in Manchester and they were very pleasant boys. Very nice. I'd like to see that as a quote. Oasis are very nice boys."

A gig at Ilford Island on June 3 saw an endless stream of stagedivers, something that never failed to tweak the band. A pissed-off Liam spent much of the set sitting on the drum riser, as an invading audience member lifted his star-shaped tambourine. The following night, Oasis were set to play an acoustic set at Creation's anniversary gig—dubbed "Undrugged"—at the prestigious Royal Albert Hall, but Liam, pleading a sore throat, decided against performing. At the *NME* panel, he had promised a great set—" 'cos our drummer's not doing it." Instead, Noel and Bonehead performed a handful of tunes, while Liam hurled abuse at them from his VIP box above the stage. Despite the set's mediocre reception, the evening wasn't a total loss. Not only was Noel was introduced to one of his heroes, Arthur Lee of the great L.A. psychedelic combo Love, but the unplugged session convinced Noel that he had to include his stripped-down solo segment in Oasis' regular live show.

With "Supersonic" still hot, it was time to put out the sophomore single. The band decided on "Shakermaker," a favorite moment of the live set, which was instantly appealing due to its blatant pilferage of sixties one-hit wonders the New Seekers' classic, "I'd Like to Teach the World to Sing," better known by one and all as the Coca-Cola theme song. "Shakermaker" was released on June 20, despite Creation's fear of a legal assault by the New Seekers, not to mention the good folks at Coke. To avoid litigation, Oasis would no longer be allowed to use the opening "I'd like to buy the world a Coke" lyric, which they amended to "I'd like to be somebody else" (though they continued to use the original line when performing live). More importantly, though, they were able to get away with their lifting of the tune's signature hook.

Noel was amused by the hubbub, and was happy to point out that he had actually copped the song's central melody from another source entirely. "I'll just go on the record here as saying that it's fuck-all to do with the New Seekers!" he exclaimed in *Melody Maker*. "Actually, it's more of a rip-off of 'Flying' by the Beatles than anything else, and anyway it's just twelve-bar blues!"

The swirling slow-groove psychedelic riffery of "Shakermaker" ran over another typically absurdist lyric featuring a retinue of characters culled from Noel's world, though mostly people pulled from his habitual status as music and television aficionado.

" 'Mr. Clean' is from the Jam's song," he elaborated for those who don't share his obsession with pop ephemera; " 'Mr. Ben' is obviously 'Mr. Benn' from the TV series; 'Mr. Soft' is from the Softmints advert who wobbles down the street and bumps into soft lampposts; and 'Mr. Sifter' owns the secondhand record shop in Burnage where I bought my first records."

Decreed "Single of the Week" in both *NME* and *Melody Maker*, the response to "Shakermaker" saw the ever-critical critical establishment bowing down before Oasis' knack for cocky and irresistable pop singles.

"This almighty second single will undoubtedly grant the brothers Gallagher access to the world of *Top of the Pops* and mass adoration," wrote *NME*'s Mark Sutherland. "From the second they unapologetically strike up a crunching, gob-smacking twelve-bar boogie you know this is going to be one unspeakably cool record . . . a Coca-Cola Classic of a record."

The band's pal Paul Mathur was even more ardent in his adoration of Oasis. "One of the hundred greatest songs ever written," he enthused in *Melody Maker*, noting, "and the rest of their set straddles everything from the high 120s to Number Three."

It soon became clear that the public was increasingly falling in thrall to Oasis. "Shakermaker" rode the chart to a high-water mark of number 11. Clearly it was the right time. It seemed that now everybody wanted to shake along with them.

six
like a hurricane

Oasis kicked off their first summer on the European rock festival circuit with a boisterous set at the Heineken Festival at Avenham Park in Preston on June 11. The crowd, already familiar with the band's touchy nature, greeted them with missiles of beer and a taunting football chant from out of the pit: "Oaaaaasis! Oaaaaasis!" Halfway through the set-opening "Rock 'n' Roll Star," Liam put a brief stop to the proceedings. "We wanna fucking play for you lot, so don't start," he sniped at the throng. "We're not fucking dickheads. We're not Blur."

Later that afternoon, over a thousand people lined up at the Signing Tent, for a chance to press the flesh with the new heroes. The fans who were lucky enough to get in were greeted by the uncommon sight of a visibly amped-up Liam dancing behind the autographing table. "You've got me at it, now!" he declared, giddy in the moment. For some odd Mancunian reason, the members of Oasis were asked to sign a quantity of Stone Roses stuff—T-shirts, album sleeves, and the like—but when presented with a James T-shirt, Noel snarled, "I'm not fucking signing that!" The signing session was shut down after just an hour, leaving four hundred punters unsatisfied.

"Shakermaker" was released on June 20, and two days later, they performed a handful of tunes on the prestigious *Radio One Evening Session*, including "Live Forever," "Sad Song," "Whatever," and the now obligatory "I Am the Walrus."

The next night saw Noel getting his first taste of respect from his elders when he was invited to jam with members of Neil Young's legendary backing band Crazy Horse. Bassist Billy Talbot and drummer Ralph Molina were in town playing with former Icicle Works leader Ian McNabb at London's King's College. The longtime pros' pre-jam advice to Noel consisted of a basic "Just bring the shit up when we nod." Noel climbed ontage for an encore medley of the Seeds' psychotic sixties classic, "Pushin' Too Hard," and Echo and the Bunnymen's "Rescue," which featured a blistering Noel guitar solo. Afterwards, the previously skeptical Crazy Horses gave Noel their highest seal of approval: "Hey little man, you can play!"

"My mum's dead proud of me," Noel told *NME* later, "because I've had my picture taken with Arthur Lee, I've been onstage with Crazy Horse, and now I'm going to have my picture taken with Johnny Cash. All I've got to do now is write a song with Burt Bacharach and I've got the full set!"

Liam, however, was distinctly unamused by his older brother's fraternizing with classic rockers. "So me twat brother thinks he's Eric-fucking-Clapton now, does he?" he bitched to Cliff Jones in *The Face*. "He'll be wearing fucking winkle-pickers and a ponytail next. He's in Oasis now and that should be enough. Our Kid's better than all those blokes anyway. He's up there next to John Lennon in my book."

But Noel was proud of his acceptance by the pantheon of greats and unsuprisingly, became cocky about it. "I can go and play with the legends and not be out of my depth,' Noel crowed in *Select*. "We're respected by bands from the sixties already. We're respected by Paul Weller. You won't see Thom-from-fucking-Radiohead playing with the Velvet-fucking-Underground or whatever."

Next up was to be the biggest and best of the festivals, Glastonbury. Widely regarded as the most consistantly enjoyable gathering of the tribes, Glastonbury is the proverbial three days of peace, love, and music, a hippie-tinged music-filled June weekend on the green. Of course the big fun at Glastonbury is always the hard partying that seems to ensue, and Oasis were perhaps more susceptible to this atmosphere than any other band who had braved the backstage porta-johnnies before. They'd been extremely busy, what with "Shakermaker" banging up the charts, and they'd had no sleep for the three days previous. Noel, who had never attended Glasters as a fan, was utterly taken by the good vibes and loose morals of those in attendance on either side of the stage.

"The kids from the crowd found me five minutes before we were due onstage," Noel later told *NME*. "I was sitting in a field watching a load of naked didgeridoo players. This kid had to remind me that I was supposed to be playing in five minutes and drag me to the stage."

Oasis found themselves with an early slot on the *NME*-sponsored Second Stage, the festival home of the moment's new and exciting young bands. On a day that also saw gigs from Blur and Pulp, the lads were given a set between agit-girl-poppers Echobelly and the British hip-hop group Credit to the Nation, and from all accounts, they blew the roof off the tent. "Today, they're the exact musical equivalent of a swagger," Ian Gittins wrote in *Melody Maker*. "Oasis lope around Glastonbury like they own the f***ing place and their extraordinary arrogance would be insufferable were it not for the happy accident that it happens to be entirely merited."

A month later, with "Shakermaker" enjoying summer hit status, Oasis made their first trek to America. They were to make their U.S. debut during the annual New Music Seminar, the premiere music-biz confab, held every July in the hot and humid climes of New York City. Noel, feeling like he'd already done the requisite stint of performing in front of jaded industry people at home, was unamused at his return to unknown status. "We're not part of all this. We're more important than some stupid industry circus."

Oasis played their showcase set at the claustrophobic club Wetlands, the downtown home of the NYC Deadhead crowd. Liam (debuting the *Musician* magazine T-shirt that he would wear at many gigs to come) was in an especially nasty mood that night, gesturing threateningly with his beer bottle, but the band simply smoked, putting forth a wall of noise that shook the airless room filled with rock crits and industry weasels.

"As exciting to watch as goldfish," declared Yank rock critic Jon Wiederhorn of his first glimspe of Oasis, in *Melody Maker*. "The music stands on its own and the lack of stage activity doesn't hinder the band's delivery. Quite the contrary, it allows the songs to intoxicate on their own without the aid of hedonistic revelry and, in turn, allows Oasis to rise above tradition and cliché. Granted the band's dulled countenance is a bit of an act but at least it's a relatively unpredictable one—look like shoegazers, sound like hellraisers."

The New York music crowd were more receptive to Oasis than the Brits. Despite Noel's childhood belief that Blondie were French, Oasis were invited to do "Hangin' on the Telephone" for a tribute record. At Wetlands, Blondie keyboard wiz Jimmy Destri presented Noel with the chords, adding, "Steal these and we'll find you."

"He's just scared we'll do it better," Noel chuckled. After the gig the band and entourage adjourned to the after-show party at the Rock Chicks'. A requisite stop on any British band's first New York sojourn, the Rock Chicks' shindig is tossed in a Greenwich Village loft by the city's leading Anglophile-cum-groupie, and is famed for the free-flowing girls and booze. Suffice to say, a good time was had by all.

The next day, taking full advantage of being in New York City, Oasis shot the video for their next single, "Live Forever," in Central Park's Strawberry Fields. With eight hours to kill before the magic hour, Liam found himself getting a huge kick out of the surroundings. He was in such a good mood that he harrassed the park's multitude of Rollerbladers by tooling around in a wheelchair. While doing an instrumental run-through, Liam asked Noel to talk someone into fetching a vocal PA so they could do an impromptu gig. Unfortunately, the elder brother balked at the suggestion of throwing a freebie concert.

"Elvis Presley doesn't want to do it," Liam groused to Paul Mathur in *Melody Maker*. "That's why he's a cunt and I hate him. Look at this, a gig would be great. Fuck the video, fuck the seminar, fuck New York, let's just do it now."

Even without a PA, the band couldn't help themselves and the pre-shoot rehearsal morphed into an acoustic hootenanny on the bandstand near Strawberry Fields, entertaining passersby with "Live Forever," "Supersonic," "Shakermaker," "Cigarettes & Alcohol," and "Listen Up."

"It's going to be so depressing going back to Manchester after all this," Tony said to Mathur. "It's like, we never ever had any doubt that all this would happen, but now it's actually happening, it's still fucking brilliant. It makes you want more of it."

As Oasis journeys went, the New York excursion was a complete success, relatively altercation-free with a positive response from the biz and the paying audience. Liam dug the States and was expectant of great things for the band there. "You go out on the street here and ask someone if they've heard of the Beatles," he told *NME*, "and they'll say, 'Yeah man, I know the fucking Beatles!' And that's what I want in ten years' time. Have you heard of Oasis? 'Yeah man, I know fucking Oasis!' "

made of stone

In London again, Oasis are booked into the renowned Columbia Hotel on Bayswater Road, the rock 'n' roller's home away from home. Still buzzing from their New York adventure, the lads spent the day cutting tracks, winding up in the hotel bar that evening. The party went on until the wee hours, when the hotel management made the fatal error of informing the band and their mates that they had to shut down the bar and get ready for the breakfast rush.

"There was a big row," Bonehead told *Vox*'s Ann Scanlon, "then somebody opened the lounge window and started hurling things out and I had to get involved, 'cos the temptation was too great."

Beer bottles rained out of the window, smashing the windshield of a Mercedes parked in the hotel lot. Unfortunately, the luxury car belonged to the hotel's manager. "The police were called," Bonehead continued, "fingerprints were taken and we were told, 'Get out, and don't ever come back.' We were happy to get out, 'cos the Columbia's a pit. It's like somewhere your gran would stay."

"At first it was a buzz being there," Liam explained to *NME*, "but then I thought it was a dive. There was a bug in the corner of my room and I thought, 'You can fuck off, this is my room.' We had enough in the end. There was a lot of pot going round and we'd got some pipes. We were drinking as well and in the end we just trashed it. Then we started running around the place and going for it. We just trashed it and things went out the window. In the end we got barred. But fuck 'em, we don't care. There's better hotels anyway."

"I can't remember the last occasion when someone was banned," Michael Rose, a director at the Columbia, said. "We wouldn't bar a band unless we feel we have justifiable reason."

Once again, the band were immersing themselves in one of rock's great traditions. Like The Who and Led Zep before them, Oasis could not seem to resist the destruction of property. The usual excuse for a rocker's rampant vandalism is boredom, the need to act up created by spending much of one's life in hotel cubicles. But, God bless 'em, the lads in Oasis were happy to admit the real motivation behind their actions: Smashing stuff up is just plain fun.

"It takes years of practice to get this good," Bonehead told *The Face*. "I've got a chair in my house that I practice throwing out the window."

Oasis got back to business the following week when they played the inaugural T in the Park festival in Scotland where they boisterously kicked a bounty of footballs into the crowd. On August 8, Creation released the third Oasis single, the splendid "Live Forever." With a sleeve adorned with a picture of John Lennon's Aunt Mimi's house on Menlove Avenue in Liverpool, the track was Oasis' finest moment to date. An inspiring anthemic declaration of the power of freedom and friendship, the song was a simple classic, the kind of tune that crosses over all boundaries.

Nevertheless, *Melody Maker* guest singles reviewer Andy Cairns of Therapy? condemned the song by slamming Oasis' old-time rock tendencies: "I started off quite liking it, until the Eric Clapton 'Wonderful Tonight' guitar solo came in at the end. Music for old bastards. . . ."

The following week, though, critic Sarra Manning decided

to re-review "Live Forever," anointing it "Single of the Week." "There's no point theorizing and pontificating about Oasis," she wrote. "You either get it or you don't.... If their anthemic guitars roll over you in an orgasmic rush and Liam's narcissistic stoner drawl kicks dirt in your eyes and carves holes in your heart... you've got it."

Getting poised to release the debut album, Oasis headed off on their second full U.K. tour. The second night, they played in Newcastle, a northern city infamous for its hardness. The crowd were hyped up and belligerent from the start, football chanting, "Soft as shite!" and "Man City, wank wank wank." Five songs into the set, Oasis kicked into the punk burner "Bring It On Down" when an audience member climbed onstage and decided to let out some of his inexplicable rage on Noel.

"I looked up and there was this guy stood right in front of me," Noel told *Q* later, "and he fucking smacked me right in the eye. I just took me guitar off and belted him across the head with it, and then he got dragged into crowd. Me and Our Kid, like a pair of idiots, jumped straight in and it all went off, fucking proper. Later in the dressing room, I noticed I was covered in blood. He nearly took my eye out with a sovereign ring he was wearing."

"I blame the strobe lights, me," he explained to *Melody Maker*. "We decided to get a lighting engineer for this tour, and we told him, 'We don't like strobe lights, because we can't see what we're doing when they're on.' So he said, 'Right,' and just put them on during the drum intro for the beginning of 'Bring It On Down.' And all fucking hell broke loose."

The brothers took a break from battling each other and dove into the pit where they proceeded to beat the puncher senseless. Where most bands would allow the bouncers to handle such matters, Oasis' tough-kid background demanded that they take care of such things. "It's just sticking up for yourself," Liam explained. "If someone gets on the stage and has it then he gets it, it's simple. People think we're up for a fight and that, but we're not up for a fight. We didn't start it, we're here to play songs, that's what we're about. We're not about fighting. We want to do the songs, do the set and get off. But if someone gets up and thinks he's a bit hard and goes for it, he's going to get it."

Considering Noel's bloodied face and battered guitar—the beloved Gibson Sunburst passed down from Pete Townshend to Johnny Marr to Noel—there was clearly no chance of the show continuing. As the band attempted to leave the venue, their van was surround by a few hundred angry fans, pissed that the gig was cut so short. Surrounded, the members of the band had to lay down on the floor to avoid being hit with the bricks and bottles caroming off the vehicle.

Following the incident, it became clear that the band's security would have to be beefed up. Jo Whiley, the Radio One DJ and Oasis confidante, was at the gig and said later, "They were really shocked afterwards. It was like, 'God! We've been saying for ages that something's got to be done about it.' It was really, really tense."

Noel was taken to Newcastle's Royal Victoria Hospital and patched up. "I've got a bit of a headache," he said, "a bit of a lump gathering over my eye but if I have another seventy-five cigarettes and a couple of bottles of gin I'll be sort of alright, I might go to sleep tonight."

Two days later, Oasis journeyed to Vimmerby, Sweden, where they were to play the annual Hultsfred Festival along with their pals Primal Scream and Verve. Unfortunately, the fest's naive promotor booked all three bands into the same hotel and needless to say, wildness ensued. "I was walking along," Liam remembered with glee in *Select*, "and this chair come flying past me, then another, then another, I thought, It's gonna be good tonight."

The Primals, sensing trouble, wisely snuck away in their tour bus after the cops were called in, leaving Oasis and Verve to pay £800 to the hotel manager in order to avoid arrest. A spokesman for the Verve explained the scene later, noting that "everyone was really drunk. The bands didn't play until something like two in the morning. Then they got back to the hotel and the bar was open. Unfortunately, they tried to close it after a while and an argument ensued.

Some bottles were purloined. You're a bit gauche if you're a promotor and you think that with these three bands in the bar, nothing's gonna happen. The chemistry was there and it's not surprising what happened."

"Everything just went mad," Liam told *Melody Maker*'s Paul Mathur. "People were smashing bottles and throwing things all over the place. At one point, someone opened a window and just started to lob everything out. I woke up the next morning, looked out of the window and the car park was, like, full of bedrooms. It was a laugh."

When asked later about his part in the constant bad-boy hijinks, Liam seemed to be in denial, or at least in full-on contrary mode. "Rock 'n' roll can be done without all the crap that's meant to go with it," he told *Vox*, "and that's why I'm not into trashing hotels. That's one thing I never wanted to get into with the band, but that fucker over there [Bonehead] is mad for it and it's sad. People go, 'Ooh, it's really rock 'n' roll, throwing your gear out the window.' Bollocks! I'm in bed when all that's going on, reading *The Independent* with a glass of orange juice."

Noel simply saw his mates' antics as yet another example of their place in rock history, though he was wise enough to know that without the tunes, busting things up is not enough to qualify a band for classic status. "The Rolling Stones were seen to be very rock 'n' roll when they started," he said. "They were always getting arrested, but the reason why they're a great band is not because Mick and Keith got nicked, it's because they wrote 'Jumping Jack Flash.' That's why they're a great band, it's as simple as that. It's the music that lasts. The headline lasts that day, and then it becomes yesterday's news. Where 'Jumping Jack Flash' is on the shelves in record stores for infinity, for as long as the planet doesn't fucking blow itself up."

His point was proved when "Live Forever" entered the charts the next week. You don't get to number 10 simply by tossing furniture through hotel windows.

solid gold easy action

Broken but unbowed, the band returned home from Sweden.
In the heat of the Hultsfred hijinks, Our Liam had busted his foot
jumping from a moving bus. Nevertheless, Oasis were fit enough to
do "Live Forever" on *Top of the Pops* (with Eternal, Boyz II Men,
and Sophie B. Hawkins also on the bill), not mention squeezing in
two big shows at the London Forum. Backstage, Noel met his original musical hero for the first time. According to *Select*, Mr. Paul
Weller, the Modfather himself, congratulated Noel on the gig, but
with one complaint: "That was pretty good, but you should do encores."

Noel, while thrilled at meeting his idol, was not so impressed
that he could quash a snappy comeback. "I've seen you do six encores
and it fuckin' bored the tits off me."

On August 30, Oasis finally released the debut album it
seemed everyone was waiting for. Noel was justifiably proud of *Definitely Maybe*, telling *Melody Maker* that "this album puts paid to all
the rumours, heresay, gossip, and sensationalism about drugs and
fucking shagging in hotel rooms. This is what we're all about. This
means we're a real band with real songs, and everything else is just

incidental. This is what will be remembered in twenty years' time, not incidents on ferries or drug busts or whatever."

The cover, designed as always by Noel pal Brian Cannon, shows the band in the sunny front room of Bonehead's flat in Didsbury, Manchester, surrounded by a number of iconographic signposts: a poster of Noel's songwriting god, Burt Bacharach, a framed photo of football great Georgie Best, a globe, a mirror, a pair of Gibsons, a pack of Benson and Hedges, and a couple of half-full glasses of red.

Blasting off with the electric roar of Noel's guitar, the album opens with the cocksure "Rock 'n' Roll Star," Oasis' defiant statement of purpose and declaration of intent. "In my mind, my dreams are real," Liam snarled, "I'm a rock 'n' roll star," the polar opposite of the sheepish I-don't-want-to-be-here attitude of nineties rock.

The hits are all here, from "Supersonic" to "Shakermaker" to "Live Forever." The record spans the spectrum of Noel's songwriting influences, be it the burning punk fire of "Bring It On Down," the Beatle-delic "Up in the Sky," or the goofy Small Faces homage, "Digsy's Diner." In fact, every track sounded like a classic. The revelatory "Columbia" recalled the glory days of baggy, while Liam's Johnny Rotten sneer contrasted the blatant T. Rex riff robbery in the ode to the simple pleasures of "Cigarettes & Alcohol" (Noel commented on the pilferage with typical flair in *Select*: "If Bolan had written 'Cigarettes and Alcohol,' it would've had lyrics about pixies and shit, so count yourself lucky.") The record closes with the fantastic one-two punch of Noel's pyrotechnic love song, "Slide Away," into the anti-romantic acoustic "Married With Children."

The critics, of course, went bananas. *Melody Maker*'s Paul Lester rated the record "Bloody Essential." "*Definitely Maybe* is What The World's Been Waiting For," he enthused, "a record full of songs to live to, made by a gang of reckless northern reprobates ... who you can easily dream of joining."

In America, the reviews were no less emphatic. *Raygun* declared the album "1994's great British rock record ... no maybes about it."

"I hope that this album inspires somebody to get off their arse and form a fucking band," Noel said. "We just feel so isolated at the moment. If we're the Beatles, where are the Rolling Stones? Where are The Who and the Kinks?"

The day before the record's official release, Oasis celebrated by throwing an acoustic in-store at the Virgin Store near London's Marble Arch. While over one thousand fans turned up, just a small few were allowed into the 200-capacity store. Those lucky enough to get in the door were treated to a set that included "Shakemaker," "Supersonic," "Live Forever," "Sad Song," and "Slide Away." They were accompanied by their new pal, Lemonhead alterna-hunk Evan Dando, whom Noel had befriended backstage at Glastonbury. Dando spent most of the set reading *NME* off to the side of the stage, but joined in the as-yet-unrecorded "Whatever," after Liam handed over his tambourine.

"We met about a month ago and hit it off," Dando told *Melody Maker*. "Then last night we colllided in Paris. We'd both been playing the Lowlands Festival in Holland this weekend and we wrote a song together called 'Purple Parallelogram.' I really like Oasis' lack of pretension, but I won't sign any autographs today because that would be impolite. This is their day."

The band took a brief break after the four P.M. performance, then returned for a marathon autographing session which went long over schedule. The doors were shut at six thirty, leaving a great many unsatified fans outside. The two hundred that got in were escorted to the signing table by a giddy Dando, who of course posed for a number of pictures with the punters. The band, with Dando still in tow, left the Virgin store at seven, en route to a shuttle flight up to Manchester to catch a gig by the Afghan Whigs. Despite a heavy police presence, their car was mobbed by fans like a scene out of *A Hard Day's Night*.

The band couldn't escape the rapid fans or the loony Lemonhead. Two days later Dando continued to tail Oasis, joining them at the Buckley Tivoli with a thirty-minute acoustic support set. After the gig, Evan turned up on the venue's roof, where he serenaded the Oasis'ed-out fans sans guitar. Dando followed Oasis to Ireland, showing up on September 3 in Dublin, skipping the next night's Belfast show, but reappearing in Manchester on September 5 for the tour's final date at the Hacienda.

Definitely Maybe notched 150,000 sales in its first three days in the shops, making it the fastest-selling debut album ever in the U.K. The album easily took the number one position on the charts, the first Creation Records product to reach that pinnacle. The record had been expected to come in second, as the debut recording by the Three Tenors—Pavarotti, Carreras, and Domingo—had been released the same day accompanied by a £2 million promotional blitz. A Creation spokesman summed up the battle: "Three fat blokes shouting are no competition for Oasis."

It wasn't just England that was turning out to be mad for it. Sony's corporate offices in Sweden were besieged by angry Oasis fans after their initial pressing of *Definitely Maybe* sold out within two days. In the Far East, the six gigs on Oasis' first Japanese tour sold out in one day, despite the fact that no records had yet been released.

They flew out to the Land of the Rising Sun. Because of the stringent drug laws in Japan, management saw the jaunt as a way to wean the band off of the hard partying they'd become accustomed to. Unfortunately, rumors of the inaccessibility of party favors proved to be greatly exaggerated. The tour turned into a nonstop bash, with the band members getting by on very little sleep. The vibe was so festive that Bonehead nearly missed the penultimate show in Osaka due to his excessive intemperance.

The Japanese fans turned out to be everything they'd been reputed to be. Noel was so bombarded by gift-giving fans that he had to buy some new luggage just to get the goodies home.

After Japan, it was time to tour the U.S. for the first time. The first full-length American tour was best described by Liam. "Mad as fuck," he sputtered in *Vox*.

"There's this thing about a white rock band from England

coming over and 'breaking' America," Noel observed in *NME*. "Why should there be that weight put around every young band's neck? Why should we 'break' America? We'll come to America as often as our record company will pay for us to come here, and do as many gigs as they put in front of us that are physically possible to do. We're not concerned with 'breaking' anything."

The tour went well, with the fans satisfied and the band enjoying the perks of the rock-star world. Girl-crazy Liam met a lass who claimed to be the last person to sleep with Kurt Cobain. "Too dangerous," he conceded, adding, "But I let her suck my dick."

All progressed smoothly until the band arrived in Los Angeles for a show at the legendary Whiskey A Go-Go. The day before, Liam and Noel made an appearance on the popular *Love Phones* call-in show on KROQ. For some reason, the callers repeatedly inquired whether Oasis were part of some New Mod scene. After a number of these queries, a testy Liam finally snapped, "Look, we're not fookin' mods, alright?" Another caller wanted to know how the Gallaghers felt about penis extensions. Noel replied that they've got one playing drums, and no, he can't recommend it. After that things got out of control, leading to the DJ leaving the studio and the band getting booted off the air.

That night the band got into a brawl with bouncers at the Viper Room over the two A.M. closing time. The entourage proceeded to Bonehead's brother's house, where the party continued until morning. It may well have gone on longer, but sometime around dawn, Bonehead decided to set up his amp in the street. There he played the spiraling "Supersonic" riff until half a dozen LAPD black-and-whites arrived and put a stop to the shindig.

Finally showtime arrived. Liam ambled onto the Whiskey's small stage alone, announcing, "The fookin' band aren't coming. You've just got me tonight." After a few moments, the rest of the band took the stage, kicking into "Rock 'n' Roll Star" until bad sound caused Noel to call a stop to the proceedings. Liam barked at the crowd, "We'll play it again for ya," but a crowdsurfer hit the stage, knocking over Liam's monitor and mike. The singer snarled at him, and after the song's conclusion, reminded the audience that Oasis are up here and they're down there and that's the end of it.

The show continued to go poorly, with Liam getting increasingly agitated about the nonstop moshing. In the middle of "Shakermaker," he gaffed a lyric, which tweaked his brother no end. As Noel glared with anger, Liam growled something at his brother. When the song ended, the singer went over to Noel and the two exchanged some angry words. Liam circled his cooler-headed brother, followed by more shouts and shoves. Finally, Liam whacked Noel in the back of the head with his tambourine, as the crowd, smelling blood, chanted, "Fight! Fight!"

From there on in, the gig rapidly deteriorated into a classic Oasis failure. Liam got more and more obnoxious, changing lyrics and making masturbatory gestures at his brother, the crowd growing bored with the antics being put before the music. Noel begged those still watching the set, "Can you lot down the front start enjoying yourselves, because you're pissing us off up here?" Liam split the stage in the midst of the set-closing "I Am the Walrus." An emergency meeting was held afterwards in the dressing room, but after an hour of heated words, Liam abruptly bolted from backstage and headed off alone down Sunset Boulevard, a towel over his shoulders like a just-defeated heavyweight champ.

Though the first Oasis visit to La-La Land appeared to be a wash, legend has it that the Whiskey debacle was the first show to be witnessed by a Beatle. It is said that Ringo Starr was present in the VIP section that night, though the fact that he was reportedly "well impressed" casts some doubt on the veracity of his presence. Otherwise, the Yank rock scene seemed to take an instant dislike to Oasis. Jane's Addiction/Porno for Pyros/Lollapalooza-man Perry Farrell walked out of the Whiskey gig halfway through. Beastie Boy Adam "MCA" Yauch regaled *NME* with the tale of his encounter with an indeterminate Gallagher, though it bears all the earmarks of Liam. "Yeah, I met that guy from Oasis," he said. "He was in some hotel in L.A. And he comes over to me and goes, 'Hey, man, you're that fuckin' Beastie Boys guy, aren't ya? Yeah, the fuckin' Beastie

Boys. We should be fuckin' mates, man, we're both fuckin' rock stars, man.' He had all this white foam coming out the sides of his mouth. Yeuch.''

Of course, the antipathy between American alt-rock and the encroaching Brits was more than mutual. During their earlier trip to New York, Liam had caused a stir when he declared the recently dead Kurt Cobain to be a "sad cunt" who couldn't handle the pressure.

Though Noel was a huge Nirvana fan, he, like many of his countrymen, couldn't get his head around the generic miserablism of the post-Kurt U.S. of A. "We got fed the grunge stuff and all of that," he explained to *Huh*. "People are sick of whining American rock stars coming over and saying, 'Life's shit.' "

Noel appeared to reserve a special bit of contempt for America's biggest band (and Oasis labelmates), Pearl Jam. "Eddie Vedder's just seen as some aloof, wincing, fucking asshole," he spewed. "He's starting to seem almost like an old fucking housewife. It's like, 'Oh shut the fuck up moaning, man. Get on with it.' "

Still, Noel was extremely upset about the Whiskey disaster. Enough is enough, he figured, and decided that if the other four members of Oasis weren't going to be completely dedicated, then, well, why should he stick around? "Honestly, after that gig I really didn't want to be in Oasis anymore," he told *Melody Maker*. "It had been building up for weeks and then it just came to a head. I couldn't see anything good coming out of carrying on. What was happening was completely the opposite of why we started the band in the first place. We were all getting caught up in a lot of madness."

Noel, as ever, viewed the disastrous circumstances of the U.S. tour through the prism of rock history. " 'We can either be the new U2 out here or this is our Sex Pistols tour,' " he told the band. " 'If you want to be the Sex Pistols, that's fine, but I'm calling it quits here.' Everyone was going, 'Shut up, ya dick!' "

Grabbing $800 out of the tour budget's petty cash, Noel packed up and got on the first plane out of Los Angeles. "I had half an ounce of coke and I thought, 'Right, I'm having this, then I'm going back to England. It's over,' " he recounted later to Paul Mathur. "I went to Las Vegas, then to San Francisco. The FBI were tapping the phones or something and they knew where I was so I jumped in a cab to the airport and I was ready to go back home.

"On the way, though, I was reading through a copy of *Melody Maker*, and I know this is going to sound really sentimental, but I saw the advert for all these Oasis gigs in England and they were sold out. I didn't even know we were supposed to be playing half of them. Anyway, I saw the sold-out gigs and I thought that if I'd been one of the people who'd bought tickets and the band had canceled, I'd have thought Oasis were complete cunts. We'd played loads of gigs in Britain but this was the first big tour. I knew I should go back to the others and sort it out."

Noel's unscheduled weeklong AWOL forced the cancellation of a number of crucial gigs in Austin, Dallas, Kansas, and Missouri. Epic's U.S. spokesperson offered an official excuse of "band fatigue." On his little roadtrip Noel had found time to write a couple of new songs which, upon his return, the band recorded in Austin. One of the tunes, the touching "Talk Tonight," was not a Liam favorite. "He wrote it while he was in San Francisco with some fuckin' bird," the singer snarled. "That's shit and I fuckin' hate it. That's not going on no fuckin' record of ours!"

They resumed the tour on October 14 in Minneapolis, and from there on in, things went swimmingly. They filmed a new "Supersonic" video for the U.S. market and recorded a gig at Chicago's Metro for a promotional CD. Oasis wound up their first "full" U.S. tour with a brilliant gig back where they had made their American debut a few short months before, at New York's Wetlands.

It had not been the easiest of Oasis tours, but then, with this band, things were never easy. Lessons were learned, fences were mended. Asked later about how the tour went, a band spokesperson was optimistic. "Phenomenally well," he lied.

nine

crashing in

After the U.S., the EC looked to be the proverbial piece of piss.
Oasis left the Colonies and joined up with a multi-band package tour
of France sponsored by the top Gallic rock mag, *Les Inrockuptiples.*
As with most of his countrymen, the land across the English Channel
was not exactly Noel's favorite place: "It's like, it's full of French
people, it's lousy."

Following a triumphant show at La Cigale in Paris, the band
partied hearty till dawn at the Le Deppaneur bar. As morning broke,
Noel, with Bonehead, Guigsy, and members of the management team
still hanging in, called for more champagne and proposed a number
of giddy toasts.

"To all Welsh bastards, especially our manager, Mr. Marcus
Russell! Cheers!"

"To Bonehead for being a fucking Bonehead and to more
champagne! Cheers!"

Stepping out of character, Liam had gone to bed much earlier, the fatigue and loneliness of the road taking its toll on his fragile
psyche. "I really miss home," he sniffed to *NME*'s Ted Kessler. "I'm
mad for seeing me mam. Mad for it. I've been away so long!"

For his part, Noel was way wired. He bid the rest of the revelers a good night (at seven-thirty A.M.!) in the lobby of the Amiral Duperre Hotel. Hours later, with the band ready to depart for the next stop on the tour, no one could find the guitarist. While Marcus Russell feared another unscheduled disappearance, it turned out Noel had crashed in the wrong hotel room. Waking up six hours late, he realized that he was going to be in deep trouble. "Look, have I missed the bus to Lyons? Bollocks! Do you know the French for 'Get me a jet'?" Fortunately, an angry French mob was avoided when he made it to the venue in time for soundcheck.

The traditional Oasis hotel ruck happened while Noel was grabbing his kip. "I found one of them pissing in the corridor, and this was at eleven in the morning," Simone Foerst, the hotel's assistant manager, told *Melody Maker*. "It was one of the brothers in the band. Not Noel, the other one. When they were leaving, I said to them that the way they behaved was a shame for the other musicians in the hotel and also for them, because the stories get around. But I don't think some of them could remember what they had done."

The band's beleagured official spokesman denied the whizzing incident, stating that "Oasis would like to set the record straight. Neither Liam nor anyone else from the band urinated in a French hotel as stated. The band has certainly had turbulent relationships with hotels over the first half of this year and they'd always be the first to hold their hands up and admit to this. But pissing in corridors, lifts, etc., has never been, and never will be, on the agenda."

Oasis followed the French trip with a brief European tour, with shows in Sweden, Germany, and Belgium, before heading back to the U.K. for their biggest tour yet. Things started out fine, with successful gigs in Southhampton, Sheffield, and Cambridge, but on December 7, at Glasgow's Barrowlands, they had one of their all-time worst nights.

The performance got off on a bad foot right away. By the third song of the set—"Fade Away"—the high living and low fun of the past months finally caught up to Liam. His voice shot, the temperamental singer punched out his mike and stalked off the stage.

"He just cuffed the microphone and walked off," David Belcher of the Glasgow *Herald* said afterwards. "He looked really fed up. But the audience got quite ugly because no one knew what was going on.

"Noel finished the song but the band looked completely astonished and the rest of them left at the end of it. There was sporadic booing but Noel said, 'Our Kid's lost his voice. He's left the building, so fuck off.' "

Noel later told *Q* just how bad an evening it was. "That was scary. We'd been up all night, like you tend to do, and midway through the third song, his voice was going. To be honest, he couldn't be arsed singing because he was knackered. He walked off and I finished the song and grabbed him and he said, 'Fuck it, I'm getting off.' So I said, 'Listen man, if there's one fucking gig in the whole of the world you've got to do once you've started, it's Barrowlands. There's two hundred screaming jocks out there who'll fucking kill us.' So I went back out and did an hour with an acoustic guitar. There were reports in the paper saying that people were booing and walking out, but they weren't. Apparently, there was some bloke at the gig tripping and he thought that the band had split up, and so he set himself on fire with lighter fluid. There was all sorts of shit going on that night. It was going off outside the gig afterwards and the riot police turned up. It was mad."

As the infamously rowdy Glasgow audience chanted, "Bonehead!" and "Liam is a wanker!" Noel played the Oasis set solo and acoustic, though he was joined by the rest of the band—sans Liam—for encores of "Supersonic" and "I Am the Walrus."

The next two gigs, in Middleborough and Liverpool, were canceled, with an official statement from the band declaring that "following an examination by a throat specialist after their postponed Middlebrough gig, Oasis' singer Liam has been advised to rest his voice for a couple of days."

While Liam was out of commission, Oasis prepared for the release of their first post–*Definitely Maybe* single. The ever-cocky Noel was most proud of "Whatever," crowing, "It's the best thing

I've ever written. When you hear it you just can't get it out of your head. It's possibly one of the greatest songs ever."

Indeed. An eight-minute epic, fraught with string-laden emotion and processed Liam vocals, "Whatever" was Noel's biggest nod to the Beatles to date. Irresistible and anthemic, the song defined the Oasis attitude towards life, liberty, and the pursuit of happiness. "I'm free to be whatever I / Whatever I choose and I'll sing the blues if I want."

"Oasis are in a different division to every other group in this country. There is no competition," Alan McGee proclaimed. " 'Whatever' is the Christmas number one, and a 'Hey Jude' for the nineties."

They filmed a segment for the British pop TV show *Later with Jools Holland* on December 10, performing "Whatever" and "I Am the Walrus" with an eight-piece string section, throwing in a version of the acoustic "Sad Song" (found on the U.K. vinyl version of *Definitely Maybe*) for good measure. Though there was a minor snag when David Bowie demanded credit—and a chunk of the royalties—due to Liam singing "All the young blues / Carry the news" in the song's outro ("He must be joking!" said Noel), nine days later, "Whatever" hit the streets to the emphatic kudos of the now completely enthralled music press.

The song was pronounced "Single of the Week" in both weeklies. "Basically it pisses over everything else," wrote *NME*'s Tommy Udo, deeming it "a song to die for, with a descending scale and a f***ing string section: from 'Love Me Do' to 'All You Need Is Love' in under a year."

Melody Maker's Everett True was even more emphatic. "Absolutely f***ing stunning," he swore, dubbing it "Single of the F***in' Year, mate."

While it was a huge hit, selling over 350,000 copies, "Whatever" fell short of McGee's prognostication. Alas, the single topped out at number 2 with the bare-chested boy-band East 17 owning that all-important Christmas number one position.

They did quite well in the year-end polls, though. *Definitely*

Maybe was voted Album of the Year by the *NME* staff of rock journos, who called the record "the mightiest debut since *The Stone Roses.*
. . . A virtual greatest-hits package." The traditionally more-
experimental-minded *Melody Maker* crew placed the album at number 4, behind Portishead's *Dummy,* Pulp's *His 'n' Hers,* and
Pavement's *Crooked Rain Crooked Rain.*

Despite their having released five—count 'em, five—extraordinary singles in 1995, they didn't receive the brass ring in the singles
category in either paper. While both lists included a number of Oasis
ditties, the year's top tune was by Liam's archenemies, Blur, with
their synthpop-disco smash, "Girls and Boys." "That's a fucking top
single," Noel said during *NME*'s year-end "Jukebox Jury" with Jarvis
Cocker out of Pulp and Justine Frischmann, the lanky Elastica leader
and, more importantly in this case, paramour of Damon Albarn. "People from my band have been quoted saying that they hate Blur but I'll
say that, although I've never been into a Blur album, I'll buy the singles
compilation when it comes out. They're a great singles band, simple as
that. Regardless of whether they hate us or we hate them."

"They don't hate you," replied Justine.

"Us hating them comes simply from Our Kid," said Noel,
dropping the blame at his brother's feet. "Sorry."

The band took a well-deserved break over the holidays, but
Noel was a veritable wellspring of new material. He wrote a number
of songs, mostly on his acoustic guitar. Liam took the time to let his
torn-up throat heal, though not quickly enough. Oasis were forced
to pull out of a tour of Australia and New Zealand with Primal
Scream and Hole.

A week before their next trip to the States, the band, sans
Bonehead (busy celebrating the recent arrival of his first child,
dubbed Lucy Oasis), attended the *NME* Reader's Poll Awards, aka
"the Brats," after the U.K.'s staid Grammy-equivalent, the Brits.

The lads were said to be "dead chuffed" by their six nomi-
nations, which are chosen by the readers themselves. Among the
awards up for grabs were Best LP, Best New Band, Best Single

("Live Forever"), Best Live Event (100 Club), Best Band, and Evening Session of the Year. The main competition? Blur.

Since their start, the London-based Blur had been the target of Oasis' ire, notably Liam, who out-and-out despised them. Perhaps it was Blur's art-school snobbishness or maybe it was just a regional North versus South prejudice, but for whatever reason, Liam and Noel had singled out Damon and crew as their primary enemy.

Noel accepted Oasis' Best New Band trophy with an expression of love for the people. "You never really get to appreciate what you mean to your fans," he enthused. "Just a little tiny thing like them sticking a vote in the postbox, if they've gone out to do that for my band and for my music, then that means more to me than gold discs and all the rest of it. Bratman, that's what they're calling me today. And the night's alright. Free beer and loads of nice birds."

It was to be Blur's night, though, as they won Best Band, their *Parklife* nailing Album of the Year. Nevertheless, Oasis picked up three of the trophies (a pewter fist with an upraised middle finger), for Best New Band, the *NME* critics' Album of the Year, and finally, for Best Single, "Live Forever." Perhaps the biggest proof of Oasis' importance and increasing power came when their benefactor, Alan McGee, took the coveted honor for "Godlike Genius for Services to Music."

Accepting their awards, Liam took his time at the podium as an opportunity to snipe at the bands he hated, like Blur and Elastica. He simply felt that Oasis' wins were a given and entirely well deserved, though they weren't all that important in the long run. "The thing is right," he said afterwards. "It's not attitude, it's not attitude. Why am I such a cunt? The Brats don't mean nothing to me. I just want to record a song and be number one in the album charts."

"I didn't expect anything," pointed out a pleased Guigsy. "We're in a band to play our music. That's all there is, really. I don't think I'm cool. We get to come here and have free beer all night. At the end of the day 300,000 people bought 'Whatever' and 750,000 bought *Definitely Maybe*. So it's quite right we're at the awards. It's quite right."

An increasingly intoxicated Liam and the rest of the Oasis table hooted and hollered when they lost the Best Evening Session prize to the magnificent Manic Street Preachers. Manic mouthpiece James Dean Bradfield received the evening's biggest ovation as he stepped to the mike and told Liam to "shut the fuck up!"

"Oasis are just soft boys," he said later. "They probably haven't had their ration of fucking chips and gravy today so they're just a bit lairy. It's like housewives who haven't had their valium for the day."

The members of Blur were mature about Oasis' attitudinal antics, coming off like elder statesmen to Oasis' angry young men. "There was a bit of a rivalry between us and Oasis," bassist Alex James said. "It was very close, it went to extra time and penalties. . . . I don't know who started the swearing but I take a very dim view of it. Still, that's the North-South divide for you."

Backstage after the ceremony, the *NME* folks attempted a peace-conference photo shoot between Liam and Damon, but Our Kid wasn't having any of it. He confronted the Blur man with his usual blend of attitude, arrogance, and antisocial behavior.

"So are you gonna tell me that we're shit?" the singer asked. "Are ya?"

"No." replied Albarn after a long pause.

"You're full of shit," Liam barked, now standing toe-to-toe with his rival. " 'Ere, 'ere, 'ere, no. I'll tell ya. I'll tell ya. To your face. Your band's full of shit. Right. So I'm not going to do a photo with ya."

"Well that's alright," said Damon. "That's fair enough."

"It is fair enough," snarled the voice of Oasis. "Arse about the award. The award's nothing, mate. It's full of crack."

Albarn walked away, perhaps wondering why the youngest Gallagher was so ticked. Noel, however, was most upset with his little brother's stunning lack of manners.

"You're fucking stupid," the older sibling snapped.

But Liam wasn't about to take any crap from anyone, least of all Noel. "You can fuck off as far as I'm concerned."

"You're just a fucking pop star," Noel cried.

"Yeah! Yeah!"

Disgusted, Noel left his bro behind. Liam, now raging against Noel, went over to Damon and apologized at what he saw as his brother's being soft.

"Sorry about this," he said, "but that's the way it is, innit? He's leaving, though, because the world is round and he thinks it's square."

"The world is not round," Albarn replied, now utterly confused.

"It is, though," Liam insisted. "It is round to me. He thinks it's square and I believe it's round. You know what I mean?"

"Oi! Liam," sighed Damon.

"You don't honestly want a picture with me, do you?"

"I don't mind," Albarn said, resigned. "I don't care."

"Well, I don't really want one with you," Liam poked. "I'm gonna have the arse and the balls to say so. Yeah yeah yeah. We're trying to sell fucking records, man."

Possessed with the spirit of détente, Noel happily posed for pics with Albarn, the two of them carrying their armful of Brats. During the shoot, Graham Coxon, the Blur guitarist harassed by Liam in Camden months earlier, made like Bugs Bunny and tried to soul-kiss his bully. Liam, distinctly unamused, accepted a buss on the cheek. After the awards, the Oasis crew set off for a celebratory shindig at the Raw Club, where a tipsy Noel managed to shattter one of his Brats by dropping it to the floor.

They hit the U.S. again, spending a month covering the West Coast and some of the South, before returning back to England in late February for the Brit Awards. Oasis were up for three prizes at the traditionally conservative, industry-approved festivities, including Best British Band, Best British Album, and Best British Newcomer.

While they took home the Best British Newcomer trophy, once again, the evening was owned by Blur. Damon and friends picked up awards for Best Band, LP, Single, and Video. The main difference between this evening and the previous ceremony was that both Oasis and Blur seemed oh-so-chummy. Noel requested that the Oasis posse get to their feet and dance during Blur's performance of "Girls and Boys," while Damon accepted Blur's Best Brit Band by saying that by all rights, it should be split with Oasis.

"If we'd won that, none of our lot would have said what he did," Noel exclaimed. "Our lot would've said, 'Fuck the lotta ya!' What Blur did was a great gesture and I wanna go on record as saying it's us and them now, us and them against the world!"

(The alliance was to be short-lived. Noel later reneged on his pact with Blur, blaming his beneficence on the evening's drug intake. "That was the E." he told Paul Mathur in *Melody Maker*. "I'd just like to say in print now that I didn't mean any of the compliments given to any of the groups at that party. I think they're all cunts.")

Even Liam was impressed with Blur's show of kindness. "I don't like what they're doing musically," he said, "but they're alright. They're mad for it and I like them for that. It's only the press who keep going on about how we're supposed to be rivals, anyway."

In spite of their poor showing, the evening wasn't a total loss. Oasis had a high old time at the Brits, though maybe too high.

"We were just completely out of it," Noel recalled. "I remember this little man coming up to us and saying, 'You're going to have to leave.' I thought we were being thrown out and I said, 'You don't understand, I've just won an award.' He said, 'Yeah I know you have, but you don't understand, you've got to get out. I'm locking up.' I looked up and all around us there were like miles of empty tables. We were just sitting there talking and everyone else had gone home. It had been over for hours."

ten

oscillate wildly

Sufficiently feted, frazzled, and fought out from their time at home, Oasis shifted their sights back to the hearts and minds of the former colonies. Another U.S. tour began in March, and by this time, "Live Forever" had topped the American college charts, with *Definitely Maybe* selling over 200,000 copies. With enough roadwork, the prospect of a gold record—500,000 copies—was more than a definite maybe. Never mind that the most popular British band at the moment was the pseudo-Nirvana, Bush. "What, George Bush, has 'e started a band?" Noel wondered.

"America is no more important than anywhere else in the world," he insisted to *Melody Maker*'s Paul Mathur, but at the same time, he conceded that Oasis were going after the U.S. with more force than most British bands did through a most simple method: touring their ass off. "It's the same thing we did in England before the first single came out," Noel said. "We'd play support to anybody and it was worth it just for the buzz of getting an audience into the palm of our hand. Two songs and we could show anyone how good we were. Now we're doing that in America and cutting through all the bollocks that the record companies try to come up with. All we need to do is play to an audience, say, 'This is what we do.' It works."

"It seemed much better for them to just play to as many people across the country as possible," manager Marcus Russell echoed. "It's all about having complete confidence that when they play live they'll blow people away. And they do."

Well, most of the time. For their momentous debut appearance on the *Late Show with David Letterman*, Liam was at his diffident best, viewing Noel's guitar solo on "Live Forever" as the perfect time to rest his bum on the drum riser. Even Letterman looked up from his cigar and took notice. "Y'know, how 'bout that Oasis?" the gap-toothed host said when the show returned from a commercial break. "Great band, great song. . . . Y'know, the only problem when we have groups on from England, sometimes they're worn out from the trip over, and as you can see, that boy—right in the middle of the song, had to sit down. . . . He's tired!" Of course, Oasis weren't particularly impressed with Dave, either. "The label told us it's the biggest chat show in the world," Noel said at the time. "We'd never fucking heard of him."

The thing is, the lads were beat. Jet-lagged and perpetually hung over, they spent a relatively subdued three days in the New York City area. A few nights before they were scheduled to play the Academy in Manhattan, Bonehead and Liam took in a set by the legendary blues guitarist Buddy Guy at the very same venue. "Smokin'!" Liam exclaimed after every stinging solo—he'd been watching *The Mask* on the tour bus. He pronounced Guy a "total geezer," the ultimate Gallagher compliment.

The last time Oasis were in New York they played the same 600-capacity venue where they made their U.S. debut, so Liam was actually dead excited about the prospect of playing to 1,500 people this time. Before the Academy, though, Oasis made a brief detour to Asbury Park, New Jersey, the deteriorating seaside town made famous by Bruce Springsteen. The day of the gig, the ocean air was cold, wet, and generally unpleasant, while onstage at the Stone Pony, the band were hot, wet, and generally unpleasant. The show was a mere two songs old when a beer can flew from the audience, splattering Noel's guitar. Miraculously, the band decided to stay onstage though Liam brandished his star-shaped tambourine like a threat and taunted the crowd with chants of "Wankers, wankers, wankers!" Noel's final words of the evening were a curt "Thank you, fuck you!"—and that sort of crowd interaction would be a harbinger of the month to come.

Back in the Big Apple, the Academy show proceeded without incident. Liam had met tennis great—and rock 'n' roll wannabe—John McEnroe at the bar during the Buddy Guy show, and sure enough, Mac returned to see his new pal in action. The Gallaghers needled McEnroe about when was he "gonna put his own record out," though of course, to McEnroe, who does in fact have a band, it was no joke. Liam delighted in Mac's lyrics, crooning the refrain, "You cannot be serious! / Double faults hurt my head!" over and over again. "He's completely off his fucking tits, mad as fuck," Noel said later of the Gallagher of Wimbledon. "Double funny and a snappy dresser."

Things couldn't stay calm for long, and the inevitable calamity happened soon after. A go-carting mishap in Virginia Beach resulted in Noel being rushed to the emergency room. That night's show, however, would go on. The band's spokesperson: "The whole of the band were there go-carting and just larking about. There was a crash and Noel split his head open. But he's a pro. He got it sorted and carried on with the tour."

The Midwest beckoned, and Noel wasn't looking forward to going back. "I hate the Midwest, I can't stand it," he told *Q*. "We sell a lot of records there and the people come to the gigs, but they don't seem to understand the band, they do all this moshing stuff to 'Live Forever' and stuff. They expect to be able to get up there and run around like idiots and they slag us off for that. But it's like, y'know, they stay down there and we stay up there. The day that I put my guitar down and start legging it over the top of the crowd's heads, then they've got the right to come on the stage."

Liam viewed the avid American crowds with a slightly more poetic eye, recalling one show in Atlanta to *Melody Maker*'s Paul Mathur: "They were hanging like bats from the ceiling and flying at the stage. It was fucking weird."

Noel's dread at hitting the Midwest proved to be warranted, as Oasis' brief sojourn through America's heartland was about as disastrous as a two-week itinerary can be.

Indianapolis: Liam gets brained by a pair of eye glasses just a few songs into the set. The band bail out completely.

Grand Rapids: Liam loses his voice and Noel is forced to take over as vocalist.

St. Louis: Show canceled on account of said voice problem.

"Most of the nights seem to end in some sort of chaos," Noel told Mathur, "but compared to things that have happened in the past, the last tour has been pretty easy."

In Cleveland, the crowd pelted Ric Menck of opening act Velvet Crush with coins, and while he might have needed the money, he had little use for a gash in his head. Liam was stern with the crowd ("You don't throw coins at our support band!"), though it should be noted that Oasis did not bail on this occasion. Instead, Liam relished the thought of mixing it up with the fans—"Any of you touch me and you'll get a smack, knowworrImean?"—finally getting his agression out by unleashing the contents of their backstage buffet table on Tony, burying the poor drummer with bananas, peanuts, and ice as the band got through the waning moments of "I Am the Walrus."

Tony's status as the whipping boy of Oasis was firmly ensconced by this time. Liam, especially, liked to rag on him, telling *Rolling Stone*'s Jason Cohen that he "never met the drummer, still don't know who he is, still don't know his name." At soundchecks Liam would frequently take a turn behind the skins, cracking, "Gotta keep my options open. Just in case someone needs sacking."

By the time Oasis returned to England at the end of March, the word was Tony McCarroll would soon be known to all as "ex–Oasis drummer Tony McCarroll." The band, of course, denied this with an official "Bollocks."

"It's a running joke in the band," their beleaguered spokesperson told *Melody Maker*. "It's been going on for as long as I can remember. But despite all the joking, Oasis exists as a unit and Tony is crucial to the band."

Of course, the whole time Oasis were flogging *Definitely Maybe* in America, they'd already moved beyond it in England with "Whatever." Now, as they returned to the U.K. they were ready to go with a new single. "Some Might Say" had been recorded at Rockfield Studios back in February, and as the band trudged through the States, Noel was swapping rough mixes in overseas packages, and Liam was raving about the tune to American journos.

"I think it's the best one we've done," he announced, before quickly doubling back. "I won't say it's the best one, because they're all good. It's just the right one for the right time. I believe it's our 'Imagine.' The words, the lyrics are deep.

"It goes, 'Standing at the station / in need of education / in the rain / you made no preparation / for my reputation / once again / sink is full of fishes and she's got dirty dishes on the brain.' Makes you stop and think."

Erm, yeah. Noel was a little less impressed with his handiwork. Why a "sink full of fishes"? he was asked. "It's because it rhymes. What else are you supposed to get to rhyme with 'dishes'?" Noel also said the song was just a rip off of "Ooh La La" by the Faces, and that he wrote the song "out of boredom" when the rest of the band didn't show up in the studio because they were busy being thrown out of the Columbia Hotel.

Liam wasn't always so taken with "Some Might Say." *Melody Maker*'s Paul Mathur was with the band when they recorded it, and he witnessed the following discussion about the first mix of the tune.

"That's shit," Liam bitched. "It sounds weird."

"It's meant to sound weird," explained Noel.

"I know," said the singer, "but weird to other people, not to us, you cunt."

"Some Might Say" was backed with a trio of instant Oasis classics. "Acquiesce" a Liam-Noel duet that, with its refrain of "but we need each other / we believe in each other," the critics quickly interpreted as a treaty between the two brothers. But Noel always said the song was about his girlfriend, Meg Matthews. The title, however, came from a most unlikely source. "I was watching the O. J. Simpson trial and the word came up on that," he said. "I didn't have a clue what it meant but it sounded a dead good word. It means being dragged into something no matter how you try to resist. The people who hear it are going to acquiesce. It's like the Pied Piper or something."

The song was written while Noel's train was stuck in the Severn Tunnel. "I knew we needed another song," he told Mathur. "The train broke down and I wrote it then. I always write best when I'm under pressure or pissed off. It's better just writing in a burst than spending months going back and changing things. Most of the best things we've recorded have been done really quickly."

Creation billed "Acquiesce" as "the first pop song ever to use the word 'acquiesce.'" Ever on the case, *Melody Maker* determined that Bostonion pop combo 'Til Tuesday had used it in their 1989 single, "(Believed You Were) Lucky." Not to be outdone, Oasis' spokesperson retorted that "Aimee Mann covered 'Live Forever,' so make what you will of that."

The single was rounded out with the storming punk-rocker, "Headshrinker," as well as the requisite Noel-sung acoustic number, this time being "Talk Tonight," the heartfelt ballad that the songsmith had penned during that lost weekend when he disappeared in L.A. A simple "relationship" song, "Talk Tonight" represented a turning point for Noel as a writer. "I haven't really written a lot of personal songs," he said later, "other than something like 'Slide Away.' It's not something I'm comfortable with. When I wrote 'Talk Tonight,' though, I suddenly realized, 'Hey, I can really write songs.' Because of all the things that were going on when it was written, it was always going to be personal, but I don't know if I'll ever write anything as direct again. You can't just do something like that to order."

"Some Might Say" was released on April 24 to immediate acclaim. "So obviously Single of the Week that it's not even worth putting a picture next to the review," scribbled *Melody Maker*'s Everett True. "You all know what to do." Three weeks later, writer David Stubbs felt compelled to honor it again. "Reviewed weeks ago, but I don't care," he wrote. "It's number one and this is worth celebrating." Yes, Noel had finally gotten to the top of the chart. "Some Might Say" had debuted at number one.

"It proves that we've done everything we said we would," Noel boasted to *NME*, "and it's as much a success for our fans as it is for us. There are ten bands in the Top Ten, and five in the Top Five, but there's only one at number one!"

The band had appeared on the groovy U.K. TV show *The White Room* to promote the song, their first U.K. TV appearance of the year. Noel hooked up with Paul Weller, sharing a spliff with him in the dressing room before a beautiful duet on "Talk Tonight." The celebs were there in force, including INXS singer Michael Hutchence and his flame, Paula "Mrs. Bob Geldof" Yates, not to mention the lovely Australian thrush Kylie Minogue. In the bar afterwards, Yates hit on Liam with all her might. Ever the gent, Our Kid stood up and kissed Paula's hand with exaggerated—or piss-taking—courtesy. The incident later became the subject of much tongue-wagging in the tabloid gossip columns, though Liam noted that nothing happened. "I can't believe it," he moaned. "She's old enough to be my mother."

The band played their first U.K. gig of the year on April 24 at the Cliff Pavilion, Southend-on-Sea—"The last time that anyone here will see Oasis play a venue this small," *Melody Maker*'s Sarra Manning noted. It was also the last time Tony McCarroll would play a live show with Oasis. He and Liam had had a bloody punch-up in Paris a week earlier, and after the Cliff Pavilion gig, they came to blows once again. On April 30, the official word came down.

"Oasis and their drummer Tony McCarroll have parted company," the press release said.

Bonehead later explained the reason behind the firing, though he couched it in somewhat metaphorical terms. "It would be like if the five of us owned a fish-and-chip shop," he said in *NME*, "and Tony McCarroll wasn't putting enough batter on the fish or he weren't frying 'em right or he was burning the chips. Right, you're sacked."

"He was being lazy," Liam threw in. "He was being rude to the customers. This is a business, this is our life. We told him to do the right thing and leave. He's going, 'No, I don't wanna.' And I said, 'I know you don't, it must be hard, but I don't wanna sack you. You know the score, we're not buzzin' off you no more, in fact you're just not our mate no more, because of this and that and because you're so fucking ignorant and you won't get your act together.' "

The next day, Oasis' management went on to explain that Tony hadn't been fired—the decision was made mutually. Rumors quickly surfaced that Paul Weller's drummer, Steve White, would be taking the seat behind the skins, which management just as quickly denied.

But what about all the recent lip service about Oasis existing "as a unit," a statement that had been made just a few weeks before? Noel wasn't having any of it. "No, no, no, no, our press officer said that. I never said that," he griped to *NME*'s Ted Kessler. " 'Oasis exist as a unit.' Do they fuck, man!? Everyone's dispensable! Too fucking right, might even fire meself one of these days."

where it's at

With *Top of the Pops* booked for the next day, Oasis were in the precarious position of having to find a new drummer but quick.

"When we got rid of Tony, we didn't have a replacement drummer," Noel told *NME*, "and everyone was going, 'You idiot, what are you going to do about the album?' Because it was just before we were meant to start recording. And I was the only one who'd heard the songs because we don't do demos or any of that shit and I knew, well, I like Tony as a geezer but he wouldn't have been able to drum the new songs. People can say, 'Oh, you didn't give him the chance,' and I didn't, but, well, call me a cunt if you want."

On Paul Weller's recommendation, Noel met with Alan White, the younger brother of Weller's kitpounder, Steve. Over a bottle of Beck's, Noel offered Alan the job of drummer for the world's most notorious rock band, handing over a "Some Might Say" CD and telling him to learn it ASAP.

The official press release introduced the new basher to the world. "Alan is twenty-two years of age, comes from southeast London, and, for those who are interested, is a Charlton Athletic supporter." A spokesman for the band elaborated, calling White "an all-round top geezer!"

Speaking for himself, White told *Rhythm* that "I've always wanted to get a name for myself, not off Steve's back. I happen to be his brother, but we're two different blokes—I'm *Alan* White.

"I went home to see if I'd had any calls, and my mum said, 'Well, some bloke called Noel Gally...Gally-something...' I said, 'What, Noel Gallagher?'...I thought somebody was winding me up.

"So I phoned him back the next day," White continued. "I thought I'd let him stew and it was him. I was like, 'Bloody hell, it's you!' He goes, 'I've heard you're a good little drummer. We're sacking ours. Do you want to be in my band?' I said I did but that we ought to have a jam or something. He says, 'No, I've heard you and you're alright. As long as you're not eighteen stone and an ugly bastard, you get the job.'"

The sagacity of Noel's decision to hire Whitey was amply demonstrated by his enthusiastic comments to the press over the next few weeks. "This new drummer of ours really gets into it and when we've been rehearsing, we've found ourselves actually nodding our heads a bit," Noel said in *Q*. "If I get a better class of drugs before I go onstage, I might fucking play guitar standing on my head!"

While fans eagerly awaited the sight of a topsy-turvy Gallagher bashing away at his instrument, subsequent concerts demonstrated that Noel was right again. The drummer—now known as "Alan White, he's alright!"—proved be just what the doctor ordered, meshing sonically with the group and more importantly, fitting in with the rest of the lads.

The long-anticipated Sheffield Arena was next, the biggest headlining gig of Oasis' life. The show was among the great Oasis gigs, raw and vibrant, proving that the band could conquer a venue of any size.

Another triumph, then, but not one accomplished without some trepidation. When asked about the Sheffield show by Q's Tom Doyle, Noel recalled "About midway through the third song at Sheffield, I thought, 'What the fucking hell am I doing here?' I started getting pretty emotional and all. When we were doing the album tour, the day we played in Sheffield, at the Octagon, the promoter took us over to see the arena with the idea of maybe playing it. We walked into this massive room, and we said, 'Are we playing the little room or something?' He said, 'No, this is it.' It was like, 'You'll never sell this out, mate!' And he said he'd sell it out in two weeks, and he did."

Flush with their status as the eye of the pyramid, simulataneous celebration parties were held in London, hosted by Noel at his elegant flat, and in Manchester, at Liam's comfortable but funky crib. Some members of Menswear and Drugstore tried to crash the London bacchanal, only to be turned away by a sovereign Noel, who declaimed, "You're not number one enough! Come back when you're songwriting geniuses!"

Unfortunately, "Some Might Say"'s life at the top was rather short-lived. Due to the curious and constraining method of computing record sales in only three formats (no matter how many may exist), "Some Might Say" dropped to number 2 a week later, while the 12-inch version of the same song claimed the number 71 position. A spokesman from Creation seemed unconcerned, stating that "the band wanted it out on 12-inch as well, 'cos that's what some of their fans buy. It does show up a few of the bizarre anomalies of the chart system but we're not too worried. We've got plenty more number one singles up our sleeves!"

Even as Oasis' relationship with its fans was solidifying, however, Noel's dealings with Liam continued their intermittent disintegration. The guitarist simply found his brother baffling. "He just starts to ask me questions during the gig," Noel said in *Q*. "Like in Sheffield, the floor was split into two by this barrier, all these people squashed towards the front, and a big gap, and then all these people behind the barrier at the back. So in the middle of a song, he's going, 'How come there's a big empty space there?' It's like, 'What the fuck are you asking me for? I'm in the middle of this song in front of twelve thousand people, you dick. Why don't you just get on with it? You should be doing your gig, you fucker.'"

Despite such internecine travails, buoyed by their recent success, the band entered Rockfield Studios to record their second album on May 8 in an up mood. With the irascible Owen Morris allegedly having been banned from his favorite Loco Studio (due to the old chair-through-the-studio-window trick), the producer and the band set to work in the Coach House.

The sessions were fruitful, if not wholly peaceful. At one point early on, Noel had walked out of the studio after yet another fight with Liam, but by mid-June, Oasis had already finished six songs for their second album. That the band's vitality was waxing, not waning, was doubly attested to by the announcement that *Definitely Maybe* had been nominated for the coveted Mercury Prize. Declaring his superiority amidst a crowd that included the Boo Radleys, the Stone Roses, and Portishead, Noel noted that "we're really pleased to be entered for the Mercury Music Prize. Of course we deserve to win it. And if we don't, it's a fix."

The word from the studio over the next fortnight was tantalizing. "The album is going brilliantly," Noel said. "We've got a lot of songs now and we'll be finishing in two weeks."

He was emphatic about the vitality of Alan White, and its effect on the new record. "He is brilliant," the Chief said in *NME*. "The sound of *Definitely Maybe* was very 'Let's whack it up to ten and go,' but this time there's a lot more depth and variety. We're a better band and this is a much better record."

Creation honcho Alan McGee was also very pleased. "We had McGee on the phone about it the other day," Noel told *NME*'s Ted Kessler, "and he wouldn't get off the bloody thing. He was fucking wetting himself about it, thought it was amazing. And you know us, we're not exactly short on self-belief but it is much better than the last one. Everyone who's heard it says that as well and I don't think it's just arse-licking."

With almost half the record completed, Liam went on an

extended pub crawl, ultimately bringing a group of thirty besotted locals back to the studio. Upon Noel's arrival a few hours later, he was less than thrilled to find "half of fucking Monmouth" in his sanctum sanctorum. "I'm well up for a bit of partying," Noel recalled, "but all these people were there and I was, 'Who are you and what are you doing in my studio?' They said that Liam and Bonehead had invited them. So I went back down to the studio and all these people were running around playing with the guitars. I don't mind, but they cost thousands of pounds each."

In a rage, Noel ordered his brother to clear them out of the studio. During the ensuing punch-up, Noel is reputed to have chased Liam out of the place with a cricket bat.

Infuriated, the Chief informed the band that he would not put up with any more nonsense. "I found the others and I said, 'We're here to make a record, not *National Lampoon's Animal House.* I'm off to Jersey for a couple weeks, go and sort yourselves out. They freaked, but I had to remind them that we were working."

With a week off to collect himself, Noel was able to clear his head for the important task of finishing the record. The band continued to work quickly, the sessions following the usual pattern, with Noel and Morris working eighteen-hour shifts while the others were called into the studio only when necessary. What became clear with each grueling day was that this record was Noel's personal vision, and that, however erratic his behavior might become, he remained devoted to finishing the project. For example, the recording of "Roll With It" was delayed when Noel arrived at the studio at three o'clock in the afternoon following a heavy drinking session and promptly collapsed under the mixing desk. Once he was revived, the song was recorded in one take.

Planning a party to celebrate both the progress of the record as well as his twenty-eighth birthday, Noel bumped into fellow northern exile and current Camden resident Morrissey. "I'm thinking, I've slagged him off in the past and he's going to fill me in here!" Noel recalled in *NME.* "He's about six foot, fucking enormous, and

I'm only a skinny cunt drug addict and he's going to kung fu kick me in the chest! I thought he was going to batter me! So we walk past each other and sort of go, 'Alright? Alright?' And we stopped and had a bit of a chat. And it was alright until he went, 'Do you live around here?' So I tell him where and then he notices I've got this huge bag of booze and he goes, 'Are you having a party?' And I go, 'Yeah, it's my birthday,' and I was thinking to myself, Oh God, I can feel myself inviting him to my party, oh no! And you know what it's like when you can feel yourself inviting someone along somewhere when you know you shouldn't? It would've freaked my mates out if he'd turned up. But I could feel the words coming out anyway, I'm thinking, Don't do it, don't do it, but I'm saying, 'Why don't you come along?' And he goes, 'Well, what time should I be there?'

"So I go home and start thinking I'm going to have to call the fucking thing off. Nothing for it. Next thing this card appears through the letterbox from Morrissey saying, 'Sorry I can't make it, but give us a ring if you want to go shoplifting.'"

On June 22, one night before their headlining slot at Glastonbury, Oasis played a surprise secret gig in the seaside town of Bath, where that day, they found time out to shoot the sleeve for their next single, "Roll With It," on the beach.

When Oasis finally took the main stage at Glastonbury, it immediately became clear that they were not at their best. Liam dedicated one tune to "all those long-haired people at the back smoking funny cigarettes," while Noel later introduces "Roll With It" with typical spleen. "Here's our new fucking song," he swore at the crowd, "and I wrote it on the fucking bus and if you don't like it you can fuck off. And it doesn't mean fuck-all!"

Truth be told, Oasis' performance was something of an anticlimax. As Simon Williams noted in *NME*, "Oasis crown eighteen months' worth of excess in all possible areas by cheerily failing to play up to the role as Festie cheerleaders that they've never been."

As ever, there were some amusing moments, such as Liam wearing his tambourine around his neck, later dancing and joking around the photographer's pit. At one point during Liam's comic display, an angry Noel spat, "Are you gonna fucking behave yourself or what?"

But Glastonbury was seen by Noel as more of a mark of their progress than a rock show for the ages. "Last year, after 'Shakermaker' had gone Top 20, I thought that we might headline the second stage this year," he said afterwards in *Select*. "And then this. We weren't on till eleven so we had to watch our step. Glastonbury is just drug-crazed, obviously, and our band are always up for a bit of that, but we couldn't get into it because we were playing. Everyone's going, 'Want some of this?' And you're going, 'Yeah, but later.' All the crew were out of it. And we're sitting there watching this clock.... It felt like four hours just watching this clock tick around and hearing all these chants of 'Oasis, Oasis' from out in the field. And I said to Our Kid, 'I don't want to be in a band. I want to work in Tescos and be out there in that field watching me shitting myself.'

"Just at the start of the first chorus of 'Acquiesce' where I start to sing, our lighting man turned the lights on the crowd and I could just see these faces as far back as the eye could see and I went, 'Because we ... *Jesus Christ!'*

In the end, Glastonbury was made memorable not by the band's stage performance, but by their backstage activities with teen god Robbie Williams. "That was the day that Robbie left Take That," Creation exec Tim Abbott told *Vox*. "When Liam asked him onstage, that was his spiritual calling. The puppet strings were cut when he went on that stage."

Feeling lousy, and well aware that the gig hadn't gone exactly as planned, the group ended up partying at their hotel and fighting with some rugby players. "It all got messy," Abbott remembered. "It always follows the same route—lines, Jack Daniel's, punch-up. They're the 7-Eleven of bands."

They ran from the poor notices, embarking on a lengthy European tour. In mid-July, though, they returned home for a pair of dates in the Scottish city of Irvine Beach. Liam summed up the band's feelings when he informed the crowd that the gig was "fuckin' better than Glastonbury, this. Not a long-haired person in sight!"

A special 6,000-capacity circus tent was flown in from China especially for the shows, and from all accounts, the weekend was a doozy. *Melody Maker*'s Taylor Parkes, for one, was blown away. "On Friday they played a pretty amazing live rock 'n' roll show," he declared. "On Saturday, however, they played what I'm close to accepting was the most exciting rock 'n' roll show I've ever seen."

At the end of one set, the often cold Liam was visibly moved by the brilliance of his band and by the out-and-out adoration of the packed tent. "You're giving me the shakes," he blushed. "I'm feeling just like Elvis."

twelve

war!

The Glasters dud had faded into but a bad memory, and the Oasis phenom grew to a frenzy. Their September tour of the U.K. sold out in record time, with a stunning 35,000 calls to the special ticket hotline coming in the first five minutes. With the record due any minute, the band did have to bag on some responsibilities, canceling a rare support slot with R.E.M. at Huddersfield Stadium.

Then came the joyous news. Oasis had officially finished recording their sophomore LP on July 25, and producer Owen Morris was like a proud papa. "It will wipe the field with any competition," he crowed. "It's astonishing. It's the bollocks for this decade."

When asked about his producer's grandiose claim, Noel had a bit of fun at his buddy's expense, sarcastically telling *NME* that "Owen Morris is fat, Welsh, and has a tendency to wear women's clothing, so I wouldn't believe a word that came out of his mouth."

The following day, they shot the video for their next single, the rollicking "Roll With It," at a King's Cross studio. The performance was attended by 150 radio contest winners, who got to see Oasis play a full set. The day was marred when the shoot had to be temporarily halted after a girl in the audience suffered an epileptic seizure, possibly due to the strobe lights that were being used.

The second half of summer looked like it was going to be great. On August 10, Bonehead finally married his childhood sweetheart, Kate, in what an official statement called "a quiet affair at a registry office in Manchester." They slated the release of "Roll With It," which looked set to be their second straight number one. But then it came out that their longtime rivals, Blur, had also decided to put out their new single on the very same day.

It was said that the two respective record labels had struck a deal in order to avoid a simultaneous release. As far back as January, Blur's label, Food/EMI, scheduled the release of "Country House" for August 21 or 28, with the album, dubbed *The Great Escape*, due to follow in September. "Roll With It," on the other hand, was planned for about two weeks later, with the LP slated for mid-October. But when Oasis finished recording earlier than expected, they decided to release the single a few weeks earlier, on August 14. Upon hearing this news, Damon Albarn called his producer and pal, Stephen Street. "You'll never guess what they've done," he roared. "They've brought forward the single release to clash with us. It's that Manchester thing of 'Come and have a go if you think you're hard enough!' "

Sensing the war to come, Damon made the decision to push up the release of "Country House" to the very same day as "Roll With It." "Yes, I did move our release date to match theirs," he told *NME*. "When Oasis got to number one with 'Some Might Say,' I went to their celebration party, y'know, just to say, 'Well done.' And Liam came over and, y'know, like he is, he goes, 'Number fookin' one!' right in my face. So I thought, 'OK, we'll see....' "

"Oasis rather caught us by surprise with their single release date," explained Andy Ross, chief of Blur's label. "We could have gone a week after that but we wouldn't. The Blur camp felt a little uncomfortable with coming out a week after. It would have looked like we were ducking out."

Surprisingly, it was Damon who fired the first verbal shot of the battle. Calling the the Chris Evans radio show from a Glasgow hotel, Albarn viciously slagged "Roll With It" as sounding like "Oasis Quo," singing, "and I like it, I like it, I like it . . . who-o-o-oaho!" to the tune of Status Quo's "Rockin' All Over the World."

The battle had begun. The national press seized upon the story, seeing the many facets involved. There was the classic North versus South divide, the inevitable Beatles-and-the-Stones comparisons (though no one was ever quite able to figure out which was who), and most importantly, the increasing power of what had come to be known as Britpop. Noel hit upon the big difference between the two bands when he referred to Blur as "a bunch of middle-class wankers trying to play hardball with a bunch of working-class heroes.

"There will be only one winner," he boasted. "Our ambition is to have more achievements and milestones than anybody in England, including the Jam."

At first it looked as if the odds were in Oasis' favor. According to a database garnered from mail-in cards included in their records and handed out at gigs, the Oasis die-hards numbered upwards of 130,000, significantly more than Blur's bank of fans. The Oasis zealots were encouraged to buy copies of Oasis singles in their first week of release, preferably at a shop that registered sales with the charts.

Noel hungered for his four straight number ones to beat Weller and the Jam's record. In addition, he was well aware that anything less than number one would be seen as Oasis' first failure. On the other side, Blur, who had never gone higher on the singles chart than number 5, had been on a roll in 1995, what with their bevy of Brats, Brits, and big gigs. For them, reaching the pinnacle would be the first step in garnering the worldwide success that had thus far eluded them.

The competitive spirit even infected the band's producers. "Blur are cheeky cunts for doing this, but Oasis will have them," Owen Morris said. "Noel wants his four number one singles in a row. Both singles are going to sell shitloads. I just think Blur are trying it on and there's no need for it. But that's up to them. I think it's on the cards for Oasis to beat them.

"I don't really like the Blur single but then, I don't like Blur. They're a joke band. They're not even Cockneys!"

"From what I can gather, Oasis have done this deliberately to set up this competition," responded Stephen Street, Blur's man behind the board. "Oasis is a good band, but I don't think 'Roll With It' is up to par, so I think the whole thing may backfire on them. . . . It's complete shit to say we've engineered this, and if Owen Morris thinks so, he's talking out of his arse."

The hype surrounding the Battle of Britpop led to endless discussions by the cream of the music scene. "I think the Beatles-and-Stones analogy is right," said Damon's lady, Elastica's Justine Frischmann, "as long as Blur are the Beatles because I've always preferred the Beatles. . . . I think it'll come down to who has the strongest record company. It's Sony versus EMI. I've heard some of the rumours about who has done what, but I'm sure you can guess which side of the story I've heard."

It seemed everybody had an opinion, from the punter on the street to the biggest rock stars on the planet. "When I first heard 'Supersonic' it blew my fuckin' head off! It did! I had not heard anything with that kind of attitude for years. That element of arrogance and cockiness!" expounded Metallica skinbasher Lars Ulrich in *NME*. "But the funny thing is, you guys write about Oasis and then you go on about Blur, and I go, 'Oh, OK, I'd better check out Blur,' and somebody sends me the Blur CD and it's like, how the fuck can people mention Blur in the same sentence as Oasis?! 'Hate' to me is a very strong word, and I won't say I hate Blur, but to me Oasis are like a really great hard rock band with attitude and Blur do nothing for me."

But it was Tim Wheeler of the Irish teenpunk trio Ash, who most succinctly summed up the feelings of the Oasis supporters: "Fuck Blur, man."

The saddest aspect about the Battle of Britpop was that neither "Roll With It" nor "Country House" was especially great.

Though irresistibly catchy and ebullient, "Roll With It" was the first Oasis tune that sounded like it was by the numbers. For their part, Blur had staked their rep on a mediocre music-hall ditty, which, though blessed with a witty lyric ("He's got morning glory / And life's a different story"), would inevitably become insufferable after three spins. *Melody Maker*'s David Stubbs reviewed the two tunes together. "So who 'wins' here?" he wrote. "No one, really. Neither band are at their absolute diamond-geezer best this time around."

In *NME*, though, "Country House" was deemed "Single of the Week," while the jointly reviewed "Roll With It" was pointedly declared "Not Single of the Week"—"the difference between good attitude and mere attitude, between shiny new POP! and hoary old rock, between loving life and merely living it, and, in a very real sense, between Blur and Oasis," wrote Mark Sutherland. " 'Roll With It' prompts the words we never thought we'd use in conjunction with an Oasis record: 'Hmmm, it's sort of alright, isn't it?' "

As the week progressed, Noel watched the sales reports and press accounts as it became clear that Oasis had suffered their first real defeat. He took off on a two-day drinking binge with Paul Weller, showing up for Oasis' *Top of the Pops* slot in a crap mood. In a classic display of petulance, the band swapped instruments for the lip-synched appearance, with Noel singing and Liam feigning the guitar.

Radio-One announced the official Gallup Top 40 on August 20, and the winner was indeed Blur. "Country House" had sold 270,000 copies, while "Roll With It" shifted a more-than-respectable 220,000. The big winners were the record shops, however. More singles were sold in the U.K. that week than ever before. Of the 1.8 million singles sold between August 14 and 21, nearly half were by Blur and Oasis. A Virgin Megastore spokesman told *Melody Maker* that "despite all the rivalry between the bands, a lot of people have been buying both records, and I don't think that's really all that surprising."

Unfortunately for Oasis, faulty printing on the "Roll With It" sleeve led to damaged bar codes which caused some copies of the single not to register at the register. Oasis, from all accounts, were none too amused by the foul-up. After an emergency meeting between representatives of Creation and their distribution service, Vital, the distributors had to cancel a day's worth of meetings to put eighty members of their staff on the task of re-stickering over 100,000 CDs.

Damon got snippy when asked about how the bar-code problem affected the outcome. "Well, it was Oasis that wanted to play it that way," he sniffed. "They started all this. At the end of the day, they had just as many records in the shops, but we sold more."

Back in the Oasis camp there was genuine disappointment, though Bonehead may have spoken for the rest of the band when he said that he could "give a shit" about the chart skirmish. He knew that in the war that mattered, Oasis won. "They could have gone to number one and we could have gone to number 102," he told *NME*. "We know that we've written and recorded a song that we're gonna be playing in twenty years 'cos we're proud of it."

The now victorious Damon abandoned the high road and began to come off as a very poor winner. He began dissing Oasis with a vengeance, finally coming clean with his true feelings. "One of the dangers with that band is they've got a lot of people around them who take too many drugs," he scolded. "That's been the way with a lot of those sort of bands whose main appeal is the feeling in the music of a sense of freedom, a lot of which is just an illusion. It's just drugs.

"I think Liam's a brilliant frontman," the singer added somewhat condescendingly. "I really do. If I was a fifteen-year-old, I'd wanna be like Liam."

Alex James tried to put an end to the feud by wearing an Oasis T-shirt on Blur's triumphant *Top of the Pops* appearance. "It's not Blur versus Oasis. It's Blur and Oasis against the world," he told *NME*'s Barbara Ellen. "People think we're not real and Oasis are, just because Oasis swear and are horrible to people. . . . Liam shouldn't call his mum a cunt, he shouldn't call Japanese people cunts, and he shouldn't say he takes drugs, and he definitely shouldn't call us cunts! It's bad manners. Intolerable. But, you know, maybe that's why we love him."

But no matter how cocky Blur had become in the wake of their victory, Liam refused to let it get under his skin. "I'm not gonna get wound up by a bunch of middle-class idiots," he snorted. "I'll just end up slapping one of them."

come together

Despite their chart defeat, Oasis were still undeniably huge.
Their first full-length video, *Live by the Sea* (filmed back in April at
Southend Cliffs Pavillion), was released to brisk sales, and they played
a successful trouble-free week of Japanese gigs. Their difficult August
ended with the announcement of a giant November 5 concert at
London's Earl's Court. The 20,000-seat arena show would at least
eclipse the 17,000 who attended Blur's Mile End stadium show earlier
in the summer. "We're taking all the seating out to increase the
capacity," an Oasis spokesman noted. "It's also Bonfire Night so we'll
probably storm the Houses of Parliament later."

Upon their return from Japan, Noel became involved with
the War Child charity organization, who were planning an unprecedented benefit album to assist the children of wartorn Bosnia. The
idea came from John Lennon's "Instant Karma," a record recorded
and released in the space of a week. The *Help* album would feature
new tunes from the best British artists, from Suede to the Boo Radleys, from the Charlatans U.K. to—ulp!—Blur.

So, on September 4, at one minute past midnight, Noel became the first artist to lay down a track for *Help*. Under the guise

of "Oasis and Friends," he teamed up with Alan White, house diva Lisa Moorish, and way-cool movie star Johnny Depp on guitar for a nifty acoustic-based version of the old B-side and live-set staple "Fade Away." He ended his day back in the studio, this time at Abbey Road, to record a cover of "Come Together" as a member of the so-called Smokin' Mojo Filters, who included Paul Weller and Paul McCartney.

"He was a nice bloke," Noel said later about meeting his first Beatle. "Has he got our records? Yeah. Apparently he likes 'Wonderwall' and 'Don't Look Back in Anger.' Is it a buzz that he likes songs I've written? Obviously."

Despite his heavy involvement with the project, Noel was careful not to come off as any sort of spokesman for a cause. "Oasis are not a political band," he explained to *NME*. "And I haven't got a fucking clue what they're (the warring factions in the former Yugoslavia) fighting about. But I know there are children, women, old people getting bombed in the streets for nothing. At least the Gulf War was about oil. Bosnia's about fuck-all. It's about fields and hills and trees and no one's ever going to win. To be perfectly honest, if it wasn't directed at children, I probably wouldn't give a flying arse about it. To me, Bosnia is like Northern Ireland. It's just men being macho and shooting each other. But when someone explains about the kids who are going to be orphans for the rest of their lives, it touches something within you. 'Cos we're all born children."

Though *Help* provided an upbeat break in the fighting, the battle with Blur was about to reemerge with a vengeance. A tired and tipsy Noel was being interviewed by the *Observer*'s Miranda Sawyer when the writer's persistent questioning about Blur finally hit paydirt. "The guitarist I've got a lot of time for," Noel said. "The drummer I've never met. I hear he's a nice guy. The bass player and singer, I hope the pair of them catch AIDS and die because I fucking hate them two."

Considering the amount of spurious nonsense that springs from Noel's lips, this was the first time that he had truly put his foot in it. A firestorm of controversy began, with anti-Oasis sentiments coming from the press, other bands, and AIDS organizations. Even the usual immediate response from Creation and Ignition Management was not forthcoming. A not-amused Andy Ross of Food Records summed up the feelings of a nation. "What do you say in response to that?" he said. "I think the whole thing's pathetic. All I can say is that they wouldn't let Liam do any more interviews with the press in case he said something stupid. This is meant to be the clever one talking. Their capacity for saying stupid things doesn't cease to amaze me."

A week later Noel finally responded via a letter to *Melody Maker*. "I would like to apologise to all concerned who took offense at my comments about Damon Albarn and Alex James in an *Observer* article printed last Sunday," he wrote.

> *The off-the-cuff remark was made last month at the height of a "war of words" between both bands, and it must have been the fiftieth time during that interview that I was pressed to give an opinion of Blur. As soon as I said it, I realized it was an insensitive thing to say as AIDS is no joking matter, and immediately retracted the comment, but was horrified to pick up the* Observer *and find the journalist concerned chose to still run with it.*
>
> *Anyone who knows me will confirm that I've always been sympathetic towards the plight of HIV carriers and AIDS sufferers, as well as being supportive of the challenge to raise awareness about AIDS and HIV.*
>
> *Although not being a fan of their music, I wish both Damon and Alex a long and healthy life.*

Even Liam had to admit that what his brother had said was a tad harsh, though he was more shocked by Blur's magnanimous reaction to Noel's vicious sentiment. "If anyone had said that about me," he swore, "I'd have twatted them. But Blur pretend they don't give a fuck. I just wish they'd be honest."

When Damon finally spoke out about the affair, he, as ever, managed to come off as all high and mighty. "When the whole thing started with them, it was quite fun," he told *Melody Maker*. "It had a curiosity value, and a novelty to it. Prior to the whole thing, we got on fairly well. We weren't best mates, but there was a sense that things were going great for both bands, and that that was generally a good thing. Now, the whole war of words has left me feeling a bit saddened. It's not what I wanted to be the outcome of the 'battle of the bands.'

"It just got so ugly," Albarn continued. "And to say things like that, you know the things I'm talking about, doesn't reflect well on them. I think they should reassess their priorities. They'll look back on it when they're grown men and just think what dickheads they were."

Soon thereafter Liam had another encounter with a member of Blur, though this time, no one got kicked out of the bar. "I met that Alex the other week in the pub," he recalled in *NME*, "and I thought, 'I'm not gonna sit there,' so I bombed over and said, 'Congratulations on number one. It's about fuckin' time, mate.' And he goes, 'Oh yeah. But both our fucking songs were shit anyway.' And I went, 'No, this is where you're wrong. And this is why I fuckin' hate your band and you. I thought our song was top.' And then I went, 'Do you want a line?' And I gave him one and it was cool. But I still think they're shit."

The Blur versus Oasis conflict was mainly a verbal one, but yet another scheduling clash between the bands looked set to escalate the fight into a more physical terrain. Both bands booked gigs in the town of Bournemouth for the night of September 18. Blur planned to fly a giant inflatable number one over the club and beam a Blur batsignal onto the venue where Oasis were playing. After hearing that their fans intended to use the evening as as excuse to get into a ruck with Blur fans, Oasis bumped their gig to the next night.

"At first we approached Blur to move their show as it is much smaller and only put on sale several weeks after the Oasis show had sold out 4,300 tickets," Creation Minister of Publicity Johnny Hopkins explained. "Their response was to suggest both bands move their shows at other nights. We acted in good faith by moving our show, but it seems their ego has once again got the better of them as they've reneged on their initial offer and are now refusing to move what amounts to a small warm-up show. So be it. We're more concerned with the safety and enjoyment of our fans on the evening, which both we and the police feel better ensured by playing on September 19."

A Blur spokesman dismissed Oasis' worry over a potential rumble between the Rods and the Mockers. "This is the usual mountain-out-of-a-molehill stuff," he sniffed. "That bloke Johnny's got his knickers in a twist again."

The Blur party line was that neither they, nor the town council, nor the promoters saw any danger in both bands playing on the same evening. Local police said they would not be comissioning extra officers on the night because they didn't view it as high risk, though they did request the start times be staggered.

Nevertheless, Oasis wanted to avoid any connection with the threatened violence. "I know coachfuls of Mancs who were gonna go down there and slap the fuck out of them, and batter the band," Liam told *NME*. "We're sick of it. Hooligans, we've got enough of that shit. And who gets blamed for it? Not Blur."

In the end, the Bournemouth show would end up being postponed for longer than anyone could have expected. Since the start, Oasis had been an accident waiting to happen, and it was only a matter of time before one of them crashed. When the band came back from the Japanese tour, Guigsy no longer showed up at rehearsal. The hectic two years had caught up to him, and the bassist fell ill with exhaustion. "None of us saw it comin'," Noel explained in *NME*. "He just said, 'Look, I'm fuckin' shot to bits. I don't think I can get on a bus and go and tour.' He was a bit concerned that we were going to boot him out of the band. The doc told him to get loads of rest. We were going to do this tour then head straight out to America and he just said, 'I don't think I can do it.' The lifestyle we lead on tour, you gotta eat well and you've gotta sleep well, and none of us do that.

"His doctor was more concerned about his diet and his physical state more than anything else. None of us eat that well, but I suppose someone had to go, and I suppose he was first. We just gave him a big hug and said, 'Go to bed or go on holiday or do what you've got to do.' "

So the September tour of the U.K. and Europe would have to be postponed and "a temporary live bass player" would have to be found. Rumors abounded that Guigsy had quit the band for good.

"The Beatles went on tour without Ringo 'cos he got exhausted," the always historical Liam pointed out, "then Ringo came back and everything was sound.

"Everyone's going, 'Oh, you're splitting up,' but we're not splitting up," he affirmed. " 'Cos we're mad for it. And Guigs don't want to split it up, Guigs don't wanna end it. Guigsy's mad for it, he just needs time to chill out."

While Guigsy took his vacation, the band began auditioning bass players. Liam and Noel found time to turn up at the Mercury Music Prize ceremonies (they lost to Portishead) and fearlessly added another night at Earl's Court. Finally they decided that the four-string duties would be carried out by one Scott MacLeod, formerly of the Ya-Ya's, a band from Oldham that had played gigs with Oasis back in the old days. MacLeod arrived at London's Euston Station on September 22, and was stunned at the throng of photographers there to snap his picture. "Is it always like this?" he asked Noel.

"No," the Chief replied. "It's much worse."

MacLeod immediately began rehearsing with the band, who were in a hurry to get ready for the rescheduled dates, set to kick off in Blackpool on October 2.

"I'm just really, really excited," he beamed in *Melody Maker*. "I've just joined the greatest band in the world as far as I'm concerned. . . . Obviously I am a bit nervous about it, but it's not as if I haven't played in front of people before. It's just, well, not twenty thousand!"

His trepidations would prove to be prophetic. Poor Scott had no idea what he was getting himself into.

fourteen

movin' on up

(What's the Story) Morning Glory? **was released on October 2,**
1995, and to commemorate the moment, Oasis threw themselves a
little party. On Sunday, October 1, they held a low-key, but still quite
posh, champagne luncheon in an old regency house in Knightsbridge.
The band, with Liam and Noel's oh-so-proud mam also present,
were feted with a string quartet playing "Morning Glory," as well
as the requisite enormous ice sculpture. That night, Liam, Noel, and
Alan hit the Virgin Megastore on Oxford Street for a midnight
acoustic set. Five hundred lucky fans got to see the pissed trio play
a large chunk of the new album, despite Liam's problem recollecting
the lyrics. They stuck around until near three A.M. signing autographs and generally having a laugh with the fans.

Asked to explain the album's title, Liam was either uninfor-
med, cryptic, or a combination of the two. "It's meant to be a plant,
innit, morning glory," he explained. "Or it's meant to be when you
wake up with a rather large one on. You know what I mean?"

It hadn't been a good few months for Noel, and the reviews
for his album wouldn't do much to change his mood. In *Melody
Maker*, David Stubbs—a longtime Blur supporter—slagged the rec-

ord mercilessly. "Occasionally sublime but too often labored and lazy," he wrote. " 'Don't Look Back In Anger' disappoints, too. It's Oasis at their least incandescent. . . . Oasis are fallen, fallen short of the stars. They sound knackered."

Yank rock crits were far kinder. *Rolling Stone* scribe Jon Wiederhorn gave the disc four out of five stars, saying, "Many new rock bands leave the starting gate with fists flying, eager to batter down obstacles on the road to stardom. But few have been as hands-on as Oasis. Their inner confidence allows the group to flaunt its jaded arrogance like a five-man biker gang."

"When the album came out," Noel told *NME*, "I actually did think everyone across the board would say, 'Fuck, Noel, what a great record!' But then, when the first reviews came out and, they weren't negative but they weren't as positive as I thought they'd be, some people in the band were flapping a bit. But I was like, 'Look, we all knew when we made that record how good it was.' "

Noel was, of course, right again. The disc contained the two previous hits—"Some Might Say" and "Roll With It"—plus a number of tunes that would eventually eclipse them. The Noel-sung "Don't Look Back In Anger" is as Beatles-y as Oasis gets, with good reason. "Some of the lines in 'Don't Look Back in Anger' come from John Lennon," Noel told *Raygun*'s Ken Micallef. "I got this tape in America that had apparently been burgled from the Dakota. Lennon was starting to record his memoirs to tape. He's going on about 'trying to start a revolution from me bed, 'cos they said the brains I had went to my head.' Thank you, I'll take that!"

Lennon wasn't the only one to give an assist on the song. "That line, 'So Sally can wait,' on 'Don't Look Back In Anger,' that was me," Liam told *NME*. "We was in America and Noel was doing this song. And I walked up to him and said, 'You know what you're singing there? Don't. Sing "So Sally can wait." ' And he goes, 'Alright,' and he sings it. He won't admit it, 'cos he's like that, he reckons he wrote it. Meg was going to him, 'Who's Sally?' and he's going, 'Oh, no one.' Why didn't he just say Our Kid said it? He won't because he needs that recognition all the time, which is fair play. Noel's a strange chap."

Though the album featured a handful of acoustic-based tracks, there was still plenty of guitar firestorm, from the opening "Hello" (featuring enough of a cop from Gary Glitter's "Hello, Hello, It's Good to be Back" to force a co-songwriting credit), to the positively inflammatory interlude known as "Swamp Song." "Hey Now" touched on the difficulties of being a huge rock band, while the plaintive "Cast No Shadow"—inspired by Mad Richard Ashcroft from The Verve—expressed Noel's trepidations about songwriting. "I'd like to be able to write really meaningful lyrics," he said of the song's message, "but I always end up talking about drugs or sex."

Indeed. The title track, "Morning Glory," was a cynical storm of guitars (pinched from R.E.M.'s "The One I Love") and drug-addled lyricism that defined the Oasis lifestyle. "All your dreams are made / When you're chained to the mirror and the razorblade." The song—the disc's first hit in the U.S.—was followed by the epic "Champagne Supernova," a blazingly electrifying declaration of Oasis' stunning life-to-date and an affirmation of their place in the world.

Best of all was "Wonderwall," a song Noel had described during the recording as his nod to Portishead (or, as the trip-hop duo were known in Oasis-land, "Tortoisehead"). With its skittery drumbeat—one that Tony never could've pulled off—and gentle, irresistible hook, "Wonderwall" would prove to be the record's shining moment, and the song that would undoubtedly be on everybody's lips.

"It's about my girlfriend, Meg Matthews," Noel explained to *NME*'s Andy Richardson. "She had a company which folded and she was feeling a bit sorry for herself. The sentiment is that there was no point in her feeling down, she has to sort my life out for me because I'm in bits half the time."

Liam's vocals on "Wonderwall" are among his best ever, both cuttingly sharp and heartbreakingly warm at the same time, but it almost didn't happen. "When Our Kid went, 'Right, you've got a choice, "Wonderwall" or "Don't Look Back In Anger," ' it done me head in," the singer told *NME*. "I said, 'I wanna sing both, you dick.' But I chose 'Wonderwall' 'cos it was right and it happened. But I don't think I could have sung 'Don't Look Back In Anger' the way he sung it. And when I hear it I think it's great."

Noel was just as complimentary in return, though, suffice to say, the interviews were not conducted with the two brothers in the same room. "Liam does a sterling job," Noel gushed. "People ask me, 'Do you find it frustrating not singing your own songs?' Can you imagine being him, having to sing my songs? It's hard for me, pressing the talk-back and going, 'Do it again.' And on *Definitely Maybe* that would happen a lot, but this time 'Wonderwall,' 'Hey Now' and 'Cast No Shadow' were literally one take. He delivers my songs spot-on. He knows. It's harder for him than it is for me. And he deals with it alright. Same goes for Bonehead or any other member of the band. They are the band. Couldn't do it without them. And it must piss them off no one wants to talk to any other cunt in the band except me and Our Kid, but it's just the way it is. Everyone thinks of the Beatles as Lennon and McCartney, but everyone also knows it wouldn't have been the Beatles without Ringo and George."

With the record pouring out of stores at an unbelievable pace, things settled down for a moment. One night on the town, Liam ran into Justine Frischmann of Elastica and, remember, the love of Damon Albarn's life. Liam being Liam, he turned the old Gallagher charm on in her direction. "I was double rude to her the other night," he laughed later in *NME*, "going, 'Go and get your tits out.' It's her boyfriend, innit, 'cos I love getting him at it 'cos he's a dick. If anyone said that to my bird, I'd chin the cunt. But I fancy her big-time! I'm mad for her. And she's one of the ones who thinks I'm a double rude lad, but if she sat down and talked to me, she'd understand. I'd take her out for a meal any day. I'd go, 'Come on, let's go for a meal, chill out.'...I'm having her, man. In the next six months, right, it'll be all over the press. I'll have been with her. I tell you.

"Anyway," the Manc Lothario continued, "I'm pissed up, goin', 'Get your tits out.' And I know she's mad for it...She told me to fuck off and I loved it. She went, 'Fuck off, you cunt.' 'Why's that?' She said, 'There's no fuckin' need for saying get your tits out, you cunt.' I went, 'Come on. Girls who dig boys who dig girls who dig boys....I dig you and I know you dig me, so let's get it on.' But she still fucked me off."

Indeed, Frischmann was unimpressed by Liam's moves. "Next time I see Liam Gallagher he's for it," she said. "What a sad cunt. I mean, I'd think he was being ironic if he wasn't so fucking thick."

The band went off for another round of American dates in support of the just-released *(What's the Story) Morning Glory?* Shows in Baltimore, New York, Connecticut, Boston, and Pittsburgh went well, with Noel's acoustic segment making its first appearance in the States. But upon their arrival in wintry Buffalo, New York, things went ker-blooey once again.

After just under two months in Oasis, on October 18, Scott MacLeod decided he was the wrong guy for the job. Despite the pleading of Marcus Russell, the bass replacement announced that he had had enough and was going to hop on the next plane back to England. MacLeod refused to talk about his problems with any of the band members, and wouldn't give Russell any real reason for his wanting out. However, the official Oasis statement about his departure reported "he was unhappy with the way things were going and didn't feel he fitted in."

A buddy of MacLeod's told *Melody Maker* that Scott just wasn't getting along with the Gallagher boys. "He was saying he was finding things really difficult and really hard work and just couldn't handle the whole thing," the friend said. "Noel took him to one side and said, 'Handle it.'"

Noel was, after all, the boss and, to be perfectly honest, the pressure on MacLeod was nothing compared to the constant spotlight on him and his brother. "He thought he didn't fit in," he recalled Scott saying. "I said, 'Fair enough, see ya later.' "

All of a sudden, the future of Oasis was in question. Obviously they would have to bail on the remaining U.S. dates, but to be fair, it wouldn't truly be an Oasis tour without a few cancellations. The one obligation they couldn't pass up was a second appearance on the *Late Show with David Letterman*. They left upstate New York and headed down to the Big Apple where they performed "Morning Glory" as a four-piece, with the versatile Bonehead filling in on bass. Perhaps the high point of the Letterman appearance was that they got to meet Captain Kirk himself, William Shatner, back in the green room. "Of course he's an Oasis fan," said the busy Oasis spokesman.

MacLeod, for his part, returned to Manchester and almost immediately hooked up with another band, this time a local combo called Saint Jack. "I compared the two bands and preferred Saint Jack," he told the Manchester *Evening News*. "I had a feeling that this was a good band. At the end of the day, that is why I wanted to come back."

Oasis flew home, where "Wonderwall" had just entered the charts at number 3. The single featured a crop of terrific B-sides: the brass-fueled "Round Are Way," a full-length version of "Swamp Song," and Noel's heroic "The Masterplan," which put question to the Oasis fans' passion for the group: "Don't put your life in the hands / Of a rock 'n' roll band."

Of course, it also reflected on the Guigsy-Scott situation. They thought about finding another new bassist, but in the end, they went back to their old mate. Guigsy had spent a boring month at home resting up, though he wasn't yet fully recovered. "The doctor's given me loads of pills," he explained in *NME*, "so that should help, like. The worst thing is I've been told to eat loads of vegetables to keep my strength up. And I hate vegetables.

"It's top to be back," he added. "I didn't have much choice. The lads needed a bass player and I'm a bass player. I thought, 'I'm that man.' "

With their mate back in the fold, Oasis got right back into the game. They played a warm-up for the Earl's Court shows on Halloween night in Brussels, and performed "Wonderwall" on *Top of the Pops* with the one and only Madonna also appearing. When the diva arrived (half an hour late) for her spot, Liam got all sexed up, telling all who would listen that he was going for it. "Man, she's super fit," he drooled. "I'm putting me snuffin' nose on, because I'm having a piece of that."

Next up was Earl's Court. Earlier in the month, Noel and Meg (and a bodyguard, of course) made a reconnaissance mission to the massive arena for a performance by Take That. Howard, the dreadlocked TT, offered his regards to the departed Robbie Williams, so long as he didn't join Oasis. A spotlight was thrown on the couple, and 15,000 hormone-crazed little girls began booing and hissing venomously until security escorted the bewildered Noel and Meg out of the building. "Imagine it," Noel laughed later in *NME*, "I've been on the terraces at the likes of Millwall, Chelsea, fuckin' Man United, and Leeds, seen it go off proper, and yet that was the most terrifying experience I've ever had!"

Compared to that, being onstage would be a breeze. The Earl's Court gigs were a definite turning point after the miserable few months past. After a support set from London's Prefab Four, the Bootleg Beatles, Oasis took the stage, and unlike many of their biggest shows, they gave it one hundred percent. For once, the whole band was in a good mood, with Liam being especially jocular. He dedicated "Some Might Say" to their "new bassist," and introduced "Roll With It" by saying, "This will always be number one." A string-and-brass section were brought out for "Whatever," which was turned into a medley featuring "All the Young Dudes" and "Octopus's Garden." Needless to say, a good time was had by all.

"It was fucking unbelievable," Noel said later. "I used to get really nervous about going onstage and stuff, but now it's like, if you can pull that off, man! I swear to God, I even surprised meself with how good it was and how good we all played. So now we do these big gigs to tens of thousands of people and we might as well play in our own front room, man, because we're just totally at ease with it."

The Earl's Court shows entered the record books as the biggest indoor concerts in U.K. history, with 19,000 in attendance each night. The VIP section at both shows was especially stuffed with a veritable Who's Who of rock greats and tabloid staples. Among those rockin' out were U2's Bono, the Edge, and Adam Clayton (with producer Nelee Hooper); Manic Street Preachers' James Dean Bradfield; George Michael; Robbie Williams; Duran Duran's Simon LeBon, with his model wife, Yasmin; the ubiquitous Paula Yates and Michael Hutchence; and assorted members of Pulp, Primal Scream, and the Prodigy.

Conspicuously absent from the proceedings was Madonna. The object of Liam's desire later told *NME*'s Barbara Ellen that "I was invited to the show but I said, 'I'm not going to go just because they're a big deal. I have to like their music.' So they gave me a CD and I listened to it and I wasn't interested. . . . It just doesn't touch me. I listen to Oasis and I don't know what the fuck they're singing about and I don't care."

Fortunately for Liam, there was no lack of birds present, with Patsy Kensit making her first post-Oasis show appearance. While Madonna might not have appreciated Oasis, they were hailed afterwards by an arena-rock veteran, Bono. "When that guy Liam sings," he gushed to *NME*'s Andy Richardson, "there is some sort of ache, as well as the anger, and it's the ache that separates some music from others. It has to be magic. His band are great.

"These bands really want to be great bands and be like the Stones and the Beatles," he went on. "That's really interesting because in the eighties you were hung for such ambitions and the indie thing really kneecapped rock 'n' roll. I really hope that there are some great bands that come out of this and go all the way. If you are shy, you become a potter, you don't join a rock 'n' roll band. I hope Blur and Oasis take on the world and fuck up the mainstream."

Despite Bono's kind words, Liam remained unimpressed. "He was at Earl's Court," the singer said later, recounting his meeting with the Fly, "and he goes, 'All right, son.' I said, 'I'm not your son, mate.' I mean, he's done a few good records, but what we're doing now pisses on U2."

Of course, the more politic Noel found Bono to be a top geezer. "He knows he's talked a lot of bullshit down the years," the elder Gallagher raved, "but what a great guy! He sat down beside me and he sang 'Slide Away' from start to finish! Now, for him to even have heard of Oasis, let alone heard 'Slide Away,' which wasn't even a single, is phenomenal enough. But for him to know all the fucking words . . ."

It felt good to be back on top. "On the Monday morning after our two nights at Earl's Court," Noel recalled in *Q*, "I'm getting up about eleven, in me boxer shorts, having something to eat in the kitchen, when I look up and there's this procession of kids coming down the stairs. I've always sworn I'll never refuse an autograph or whatever, so I open the door and say, 'Do you want a cup of tea, then?' I swear to God, man, it was like the chimps' tea party in here, all these kids, me with the Tetley's and the kettle. Then this thought comes to me. Mark Chapman. He's here. I'm gonna get shot! So I say, 'Er, sorry, you'll have to go now, a car's coming to take me to the airport, I forgot.' I'm thinking, Last time I'm gonna do this. We've got to get out of here, get a place of our own. It's too much."

They set off to Europe to play the dates postponed by Guigsy's holiday, making stops in France and Holland. In late November, Liam turned up at the MTV Europe Awards in Paris, and soon got into another ruck. Hanging about backstage, Our Kid found himself on the receiving end of INXS frontman Michael Hutchence's verbal abuse. The tiff apparently started over Liam's nasty public cracks about Hutchence's honey, Paula Yates. Using his head for a change, Liam didn't allow the insults to get to him and he tried to leave what was turning into a bad scene indeed. But Hutchence persisted, calling Liam "a chicken," until the voice of Oasis finally reached the point where he had all he could stand, and he couldn't stand any more. Liam simply told Hutchence that if he didn't back off that instant, he would smash his pretty face with a fire extinguisher. Wisely, Hutchence put an end to the fighting (though it must have picked up again later that night at the after-show party, because Liam ended up twatting Hutchence in the head, resulting in his being booted from the bash).

With a new enemy fresh in his mind, Liam also paid a pre-show visit to his old pal Damon Albarn. "He was in his dressing room," he cackled in *Melody Maker*, "and I walked in in slow motion and went, 'Heelloooo Daaaaaaymooon, I'm from Manchesteeeeeur. Weeee taaaaaaaaaalk reeeeeeally slooooooowly ooooop Nooorth 'cos we'eeeeeere reeeally stoooooopid. Have a good gig.' It really freaked him out and they played shit. I went up to him afterwards and said, 'You were shit.' He went, 'What do you mean, shit?' And I went, 'Well, just, like, shit. Your album's shit as well.' So Damon goes, 'Well I think your album's shit as well.' And I was like, Brilliant, let me buy you a drink. At last it's out in the open. Let's be honest with each other. Oh, and by the way, how's your missus? It's good that there's a rivalry, but it ought to be out in the open. Graham out of Blur's a nice bloke, it's the rest that are cunts."

With "Wonderwall" nestled comfortably in the upper reaches of the charts—though it never reached the all-important number one—Oasis returned to the U.K. They played a big home-town show at Manchester's NYMEX Arena and made a triumphant, though Liam-less, appearance on the *Later with Jools Holland* TV show. Word was, the singer had lost his voice due to some excessive carousing and gallivanting. (Quoth the Oasis spokesman: "He's got a bit of a flu.") Liam attempted to vocalize on a cover of Slade's classic "Cum On Feel the Noize," which an eyewitness described as "a shit version, so Liam just said, 'Fuck it, do it again without me,' and went for a sleep in the dressing room." Noel, always ready to croon a tune, took over the vocal duties and sang it instead, and threw in fine string-section–accompanied versions of "Wonderwall" and "Round Are Way" for good measure.

Singing three songs just wasn't enough for Noel, so he made a couple of surprise appearances as opening act for Paul Weller at London's Brixton Academy. The crowd went mad as Noel took the stage and announced that "I only came here for a drink." He played a number of unplugged Oasis hits, as well as a version of "You've Got to Hide Your Love Away." The Beatles motif continued later with Noel joining Weller for an encore rave-up of "Come Together," in a semi-reunion of the Smokin' Mojo Filters.

Happy at last, Oasis then headed off to the States for some makeup shows from the last, ill-fated tour, as well as a number of radio-sponsored, multi-band Christmas shows. The constant efforts in the Colonies looked like they were finally paying off. (*What's the Story*) *Morning Glory?* was starting to sell and "Wonderwall" was showing all the earmarks of a potential breakthrough hit.

While they were in America, something odd happened back home. The supercool indie label, Fierce Panda, released a single dubbed "Wibbling Rivalry," credited to "Oas*s." Billed as "fourteen minutes of verbal mayhem," the 7-inch consisted of a recording of the Gallagher Brothers' classic blow-up in front of journo John Harris so long ago. The A-side, or the "Noel side" featured "a lot of swearing and cussing," while the flip, "Liam side," contained "even more swearing and cussing."

NOEL : *He's on about a reputation, about getting thrown off fuckin' ferries. Getting thrown off ferries and getting deported is summat that I'm not proud about.*

LIAM : *Well I am, la.*

NOEL : *Alright. Well if you're proud about getting thrown off ferries, why don't you go and support West Ham and get the fuck out of my band and go and be a football hooligan? We're musicians, right? Not football hooligans.*

LIAM : *You're only gutted 'cos you was in bed fuckin' reading your fuckin' books—*

NOEL : *Not at all. Here's a quote for you from my manager, Marcus Russell—*

LIAM : *He's a fuckin' . . . another fuckin'—*

NOEL : *Shut up, you dick. He gets off the ferry after getting fuckin' deported. I'm left in Amsterdam with me dick out like a fuckin' spare prick at a fuckin' wedding . . .*

LIAM : *It was a bad move—*

NOEL : *Shut up! Shut up! He gets off the ferry and Marcus says, "What the fuck are you doing?" These lot think it's rock 'n' roll to get thrown off a ferry. . . .*

LIAM : *No I don't.*

NOEL : *Shut up. These lot think it's rock 'n' roll to get thrown off. . . .*

LIAM : *I don't.*

NOEL : *Shut up, man! These lot think it's rock 'n' roll to get thrown off a ferry. Do you know what my manager said to him? He said, "Nah. Rock 'n' roll is doing your gig, playing your music, coming back and saying you blew 'em away." Not getting thrown off the ferry like some fuckin' scouse schlepper with handcuffs. That's football hooliganism, and I won't stand for it. And listen, they all got fined a thousand pounds each.*

LIAM : *We didn't at all. You can stick your thousand pounds right up yer arse till it comes out your fuckin' big toe.*

And so forth. The single ended up being the highest-charting interview disc ever, actually reaching number 52. Despite the indie label's obvious worries (the words "Is this strictly legal?" and "See you in court!" were etched in the vinyl's out groove) a lawsuit was avoided presumably due to the Gallaghers' sense of humor, as well as their massive egos, seeing how Fierce Panda was sure to thank "the greatest band in Britain" on the sleeve.

On a more financially beneficial note, a goofy cover version of "Wonderwall" was looking like a bigger hit than the original. In the hands of the faux-cheesy easy-listening combo known as Mike Flowers Pops, the love song to Meg became the Burt Bacharach song of Noel's dreams. Not just a joke version, the single shot up the chart, looking dead set to take the coveted Christmas number one slot. Noel was amused and enriched by the track, so he paid a visit to a Pops performance. "Noel was down the front," the blond-bewigged Flowers recounted after, "chanting, 'Oasis! Oasis!' We're just bringing out an aspect which isn't in their version, making it more personal. We're not being ironic. It's just a nice song. Good melody."

Alas, Mike Flowers Pops' "Wonderwall" wasn't quite nice enough to reach the top of the chart. It hit as far as number 2, stopped on Christmas week by Michael Jackson's treacly "Earth Song." No matter, though. For Oasis, the cover's success was all good fun (and a few thousand pounds in Noel's pocket as a bonus), but mostly it showed just how prevalent Oasis had become in Britain. After all the bad moments in 1995—the sacking of Tony, Glastonbury, the loss to Blur, the temporary departure of Guigsy and countless canceled shows—it looked like the year was going to end on a up note.

To celebrate this most tumultuous year, Creation Records threw a grand Christmas party for them at the Halcyon Hotel in Holland Park. At midnight, Alan McGee clinked a glass and called for silence. He told the invited guests that since Oasis had given Creation their most successful year ever, it was only fair that they be rewarded. McGee then presented each band member with a gift. To Alan White, he gave a toy Mini Cooper automobile, as well a check to cover the cost of a full-size model. Bonehead was gifted with a fancy Rolex watch and a card informing him that a new piano had been delivered to his front room in Manchester. Guigsy also got a watch, as well as an expensive membership in a gym, McGee thinking of his investment's health as always. Liam, too, received a Rolex, plus a box of designer clothes and a Gibson Epiphone facsimile of John Lennon's guitar. McGee then made a big show of having run out of boxes and brought Noel out to the front of the hotel. Sitting at the curb was a vintage chocolate-brown Rolls-Royce Corniche. "There it is, man," McGee said.

"What?" said the confused Noel.

"That car, the one I promised you when you signed," the Creation Santa exclaimed. "It's yours, man!"

"What am I going to do with it?" the astonished Noel asked. "I can't drive."

Creation had indeed agreed to give Noel a Rolls, but no one really believed it was going to happen so quickly. It was a major moment in the life of Noel Gallagher. Here was petrol-guzzling proof that all of his dreams had come true. According to the ever-present Oasis spokesman, "Alan said it was the first time he's ever seen Noel Gallagher lost for words."

fifteen

wanna be startin' something

Though they might have lost the initial battle, the year-end readers' polls found Oasis to have been the real winner of the war with Blur (not to mention the fact that *(What's the Story) Morning Glory?* had outsold *The Great Escape* by a huge margin). The *Melody Maker* critics' list named them Best Band, plus awarded them the top honor for Best Album and Best Single ("Wonderwall," with "Some Might Say" and "Roll With It" coming in at 3 and 4, respectively). In addition, Noel took the Loudmouth of the Year—with Liam in second place—and incredibly, Oasis were voted the People You'd Like to See More Of.

They played a few makeup shows in Germany and then hit Edinburgh for two nights. Following the second Scottish gig, Liam turned up at a local club to see an Oasis copy band called the Gallaghers. After their set, a bemused Liam joined his copycats for a few cocktails, offering them a support slot and telling them to milk his approval for everything they can get.

The Gallaghers weren't the only Oasis tribute band touring about Britain. The Glaswegian-based No Way Sis were also capitalizing on the stardom of Oasis, though they attempted a more realistic representation by wearing thick false eyebrows. After Liam's blessing of the Gallaghers, No Way Sis manager Russell Nomark (get it?) began a war of words with the competition. He said that the Gallaghers were "more like pub rock," and pointed out that "they don't even look like Oasis. How can you have a tribute band who don't look like the originals? It's a bit like sending out four baldies and passing them off as Led Zeppelin."

Nevertheless, both Liam and Noel were tickled pink by their mimics. A Creation spokesman said that the competition between the two copy bands was "a compliment to the band and their songs."

At this point, while most of the the band members were settled down with significant others, Liam began stepping out with a vengeance. He had a brief dalliance with supermodel Helena Christensen, and then began seeing actress Patsy Kensit, the estranged wife of Simple Minds leader Jim Kerr and ex-wife of Big Audio Dynamite's Dan Donovan. Kensit had first become famous for her role as the luscious Crepe Suzette in the ill-fated movie version of Colin MacInnes' definitive Brit teen novel, *Absolute Beginners*. After that she trilled in the dreadful eighties band, Eighth Wonder, and made a number of not-very-good films, but she seemed to have her best success at being a rock star's lover.

Though they had met in a photo-op sort of way after Earl's Court, Liam and Patsy didn't truly connect until they hooked up on a wild December night on the town with mutual friends in Manchester. After the long evening, the two parted with a short kiss and an exchange of phone numbers. "Fucking hell," Liam exclaimed to his friends the next morning, "Patsy-fucking-Kensit! I've got her fucking number! And she's mad for it!"

"The first two or three dates we just talked and talked," Patsy told *The Face*. "And he listened to me. We talked about what he wanted from a relationship, and about music—he'd play loads of stuff—and a lot about John Lennon."

Still, as Liam and Patsy began their romance, the British tabloids went berserk chronicling Our Kid's amorous adventures. *News of the World* ran a tale headlined "Oasis Rat Liam Loo-ved Me and Left Me!" in which "pop singer" Berri alleged that after she rescued Liam from a swarm of groupies at a Manchester party, he offered to take her to the South of France, but only took her to the ladies' loo where they had "passionate" sex. Berri called Liam a "real life sex god," adding that "he was very naughty and very adventurous."

After the Patsy affair was splashed across the pages in every tab in England, *News of the World* ran with another story of Liam's love life. They declared that Gallagher was "two-timing Patsy with a sexy French singer," one Sandrine de la Plage, who claimed that he had offered her a French holiday, as well as a trip to the toilet. According to the report, de la Plage refused to make love in a stall, so the pair went back to his hotel room where Liam "turned out to be a total flop in bed."

Without commenting on the validity of these stories, Liam finally declared his feelings for Patsy in public. *The Sun* reported that Liam had referred to his paramour as a "top girl," adding, "We're perfect for each other. We both love getting out of our heads."

Wherever Liam and Noel went, paparazzi were sure to follow. The Gallaghers took the tabloid hubbubs with a grain of salt. "I think it just shows how big they are," pointed out the official Oasis spokesman. "The tabloids are always interested in who people are shagging, particularly if they're in the public eye, so that's going to happen."

"You have to deal with it," Noel explained. "You know, deny nothing, man, because I've got nothing to be ashamed of."

Meanwhile, ex-drummer Tony McCarroll began pursuing his legal options. He filed a writ at London's High Court naming Noel, Liam, Bonehead, and Guigsy as defendants. The suit alleged that Tony was fired by Bonehead via phone on April 28, 1995, with the official sack coming later that day from Marcus Russell. McCarroll sought royalties and damages, claiming that Oasis had signed contracts with Sony Music Entertainment U.K. on October 22, 1993, with all five members agreeing to record up to five records. According to the writ though, Noel allegedly asked Tony not to sign the deal, but to instead make a separate contract as a "session musician." The writ went on to say that "the expulsion was orchestrated by the first defendant"—i.e., Noel—and that "Tony McCarroll and the defendant did not get on with each other on a personal level."

Tony's attorney released a statement saying that "there is no evidence to suggest his drumming was in any way inadequate and he still practices. His drumming is not the issue. It is the contract that is the issue." The lawyer went on to say that the drummer's departure effectively ended the five founding members' original management deal. Among McCarroll's requests were a thorough once-over of Oasis' accounts, a declaration that the original partnership had been dissolved, a declaration that he was unlawfully fired, plus compensation, court costs, and interest—an amount covering upwards of half a million pounds.

Even with this unpleasant bump in the road, things were going swimmingly. Noel hosted his own radio show on BBC. *Gallagher's London Radio* featured guest appearances by Paul Weller as well as a prerecorded interview with Robbie Williams. The ex–Take That throb regaled Noel and the listeners with the tale of his post-Glastonbury meeting with the other four members of the boy-band. "I went in and said, 'Lads, I've had a great time. I met Oasis, I met Paul Weller, all of them lot,' and they went, 'You're sacked!' "

A monster gig at Manchester's Maine Road Stadium—home of the beloved Man City football squad—was put on sale in early February and all 40,000 tickets for the April 27 concert were sold in under three hours, breaking all previous sales records. Fans had lined up overnight in bad weather, and over a thousand were turned away. British Telephone reported "significant problems" putting through the estimated one million calls made in the first hour of sales.

That shining moment was followed by the 1996 awards season, kicking off with *NME*'s reader-voted Brats. On his way to the ceremonies, Noel decided that he was bit hungry, so his chauffeur pulled the choco-brown Rolls up to a McDonald's where the man of the people himself went in and got a Big Mac.

Which was a fitting meal, seeing how that night at the Brats

Oasis were big indeed. They took home the trophies for Best Live Act, Best Band, Best LP, and Best Single ("Wonderwall"). In addition, Liam was declared Most Desirable Human Being, while his arch-foe Damon Albarn was named Git of the Year, thus putting a final nail in the coffin of Blur's ignominious defeat. Noel accepted the batch of honors with a particularly blunt speech. "It's hard to be humble at times like this so I won't try," he smiled. "You're all shit!"

After the fact, he was far more humble. "I feel honored that our band was voted Best Album, Best Band, Best Group, Best-looking Band, Best Dressed, Best Manc band, best everything, and it was voted for by fans and not stupid journalists," Noel said. "I don't like people who come to awards ceremonies and say these awards don't mean anything. It's like, having awards doesn't make you any better or any worse but it would really do my head in if I went out on a Tuesday afternoon in the pouring rain to the postbox to vote for my favorite band and then they went up and said they weren't bothered. That's tragic."

The Brats were soon followed by the Brits, which were held at Earl's Court. This was to be the year that the Brits finally caught up with pop music, so Oasis, Blur, Pulp, et al. were all up for awards. The evening turned out to be more exciting than anyone might have expected when Jarvis Cocker, the singer-auteur of Pulp, made a surprise attack on the stage during Michael Jackson's appalling production number. Surrounded by waifs of all colors, Jacko kissed a rabbi then ascended heavenward with his arms outstretched. The slightly tipsy Cocker left his seat, climbed onstage and expressed the feelings of the Britpop community by turning his back to the audience, bending over, and wagging his bum.

"We said to him afterwards that he should have done more," Noel said later. "We told him he should've fuckin' nailed that cunt Jackson. He were that fuckin' close, man. . . . He should've fuckin' headbutted the cunt. That's what 99 percent of the people on the street would've done. . . . People fuckin' hate cunts like him, Annie Lennox, and Phil Collins. And if they don't, they fuckin' should."

(Asked later about Jacko's messiah complex, Noel wondered, "Who does he think he is? Me?")

Though the Oasis gang couldn't top Jarvis's spectacular statement, they did manage to get into some trouble. When they won Best Video for "Wonderwall," a bearded and leather-anoraked Liam took to the podium, where he engaged in some verbal fisticuffs with trophy presenter Michael Hutchence. Liam larfed that Hutchence owed him a slap (either for his comments about Paula Yates, or the recent photo of Patsy with her hand down Hutchence's pants) but they kissed instead. Noel, however, was not as forgiving. He grabbed the mike and exclaimed, "Has-beens shouldn't be presenting fucking awards to gonna-be's. . . . I have nothing to say except for I am extremely rich and you're not!"

"Well, he had it coming, didn't he?" Noel said later about his attack on Hutchence. "Fuckin' tosser. He'd been saying stuff about me, so I thought I should say a couple of things about him. At the Brats, he said his next album would piss all over anything that Noel Gallagher could do. He said I couldn't even touch the stuff that he was writing. Well, in my opinion anyone who wants to pick a fight with me is gonna fuckin' get one. Everybody knows that. I don't make a secret of it, know what I mean?"

For his part, Michael Hutchence took the abuse like a man. "Well, I loved their attitude," he said after the ceremony. "I didn't mind at all. I think they're great and I love the way they behave and I didn't care. That's just the way they are."

(Backstage, the INXS leader changed his tune and found himself in a mix-up with Guigsy. "Hutchence kept poking him in the shoulder," an eyewitness said, "just trying to be a wise guy. Guigsy threatened to take him outside and sort him out, but then he said he didn't want to waste a fight on him.")

The Oasis lads were in an especially ornery mood this night. Upon taking the Best Band award from presenter Pete Townshend, Noel announced that "there are seven people in this room tonight who are give a little hope to young people in this country": Oasis, Alan McGee, and the Labour Party's Tony Blair, who was on hand to present a Lifetime Achievement Award to David Bowie. Noel then urged everyone to vote Labour in the coming elections, shouting, "Power to the people!"

Liam accepted Best Album from Lenny Kravitz by leading Oasis through an a capella rendition of Blur's "Parklife," with the lyric amended to "Shitelife." After that, he refused to leave the stage, swearing that "anyone who thinks they're hard enough to take us off the stage can come up now!" He concluded his remarks by mock-thrusting his Brit Award up his bum.

"Michael Hutchence, what's he doing presenting me with an award?" Noel groused later. "You should have had Johnny Marr up there, you should have had Keith Richards, Paul McCartney.

"And what is Michael Jackson doing here," he went on, "apart from to further his own career? That's crass, man. . . . Annie Lennox, Best Female Solo Artist, what's all that about? Annie Lennox? Do me a fucking favor. What about fucking Bjork and PJ Harvey? Annie Lennox? What's she done? Ever, in her entire life? Ever? Ever? Ever? Ever? Let alone this fucking year? It's a fucking scandal, man. We'll come here, we'll get pissed, and we'll take the awards. But I tell you what, man, they're fucking presented by idiots."

Between the Jarvis versus Jacko furor and the irascible, unairable antics of Oasis, the Brits were a media sensation. The always-excitable papers screamed about these ill-mannered pop stars, at the same time delighting in the hijinks. In spite of all the attention, the TV broadcast, which aired the following night, deleted Cocker's assault as well as the bulk of the Oasis acceptance speeches.

"What I don't understand about all this," Noel questioned in *NME*, "is that in England a few bods from Manchester go up onstage and say a couple of swear words and the whole fuckin' country goes mad. It's like a national fuckin' scandal. They say we're a disgrace to our country. It's on the six o'clock news and all that. It's mad, I mean are people so fuckin' stuck up and uptight that they get shocked by this sort of stuff? I mean, what are we supposed to do? Get up there like fuckin' Annie Lennox and say, 'Oh, I'm so, so honored to be accepting this award'? Fuck that. You gotta get in there and give it a bit of stick, know what I mean?"

In their wake Oasis left behind a table covered with hundreds of empty bottles. After the event, Guigsy and Alan attended the official Brits after-party, while the rest of the gang partied into the wee hours at the Landmark Hotel with their pal, Robbie Williams.

A spokesman for the Brits noted, "They're rock 'n' roll stars and if they want to be loud, that's fine by us. I think everybody feels that way."

**Gallagher, Gallagher, and Dando at London's Virgin megastore:
"Evan 'elp us!"** (KEVIN CUMMINS/Lfi-CUM)

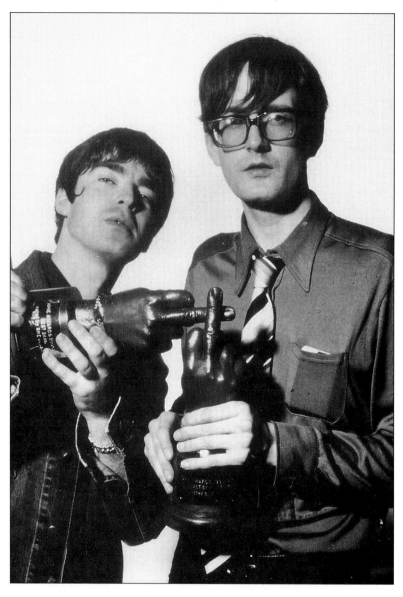

**Noel and Pulp's Jarvis Cocker at the 1996 Brat Awards:
"It's good to be Number One!"** (KEVIN CUMMINS/Lfi-CUM)

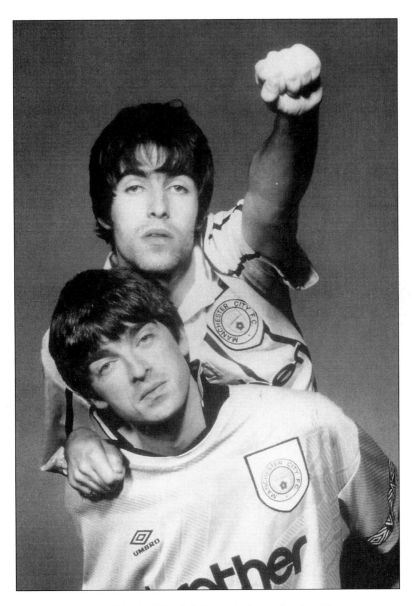

Liam and Noel: "He ain't 'eavy, he's me brother!"
(KEVIN CUMMINS/Lfi-CUM)

Liam at Knebworth: "I've got no pants on."
(COLIN STREATER/Lfi-CS)

Liam and Noel at Loch Lomond: "I know it was you, Fredo. . . ."
(ILPO MUSTO/Lfi-IM)

Liam on the pitch: "These two are for you, Damon!"
(COLIN MASON/Lfi-CM)

Oasis: "The kids are alright . . . except maybe for the one on the left."
(TOM SHEEHAN/Lfi-TS)

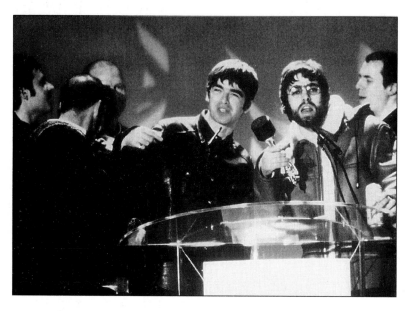

Oasis at the 1996 Brits: "You like us! You really like us!"
(DAVID FISHER/Lfi-DF)

a rush and a push and the land is ours

To celebrate the single release of "Don't Look Back in Anger," and its instant rise to the number one position, all five members appeared as hosts of *Top of the Pops* where they performed an unprecedented two tunes. "Best band in the world," Noel said to kick off the proceedings. "Live and exclusive. And it's not Blur."

The joke was, Blur were on the show as well, with their "Stereotypes" single going no higher than number 7. "The war was won tonight," Noel boasted to *Select*'s Paolo Hewitt. "You know, I've heard he's doing a Brian Wilson at the moment, is Damon. Apparently, he can't stop playing *Morning Glory*, trying to figure out how to beat us. But you see, the thing is, all the pressure is on them now. They've got to come back with a great album. Whereas we've got all the time in the world."

Did Noel go say hello to his foe backstage? "Did I, fuck," he snorted. "I can't even be in the same room as him."

Don't look back in anger, indeed. Anyway, the new single was backed by a scrappy version of "Cum On Feel the Noize," this time with Liam at the mike, as well as a perky little number called "Step Out." Originally slated as a *(What's the Story) Morning Glory?*

cut, "Step Out" was left off of the album because of its indisputable similarities to a certain R&B classic.

"Obviously it's fucking 'Uptight' by Stevie Wonder," Noel told *NME*'s Keith Cameron. "We went to get the clearance and we were going, 'We'll credit you, man, don't fuckin' worry about that,' and the cheeky bastard wanted fuckin' six points on the album.... So anyway, we said, 'Do you know how much money you're gonna get? Nothing, because it's not going on the album, so you can fuck right off!' "

With the U.K. and Europe in their pocket they ventured off yet again to America for another go-round at Noel's dreaded Midwest. By now "Wonderwall" was a radio staple and *(What's the Story) Morning Glory?* was banging up the album charts. Oasis looked certain to replicate their success in a country where no British band had made it in years.

"I think we're by far the most accessible English band since the Sex Pistols," Noel bragged to *Alternative Press*. "I think the American public will always find something magical about five English boys with funny haircuts and funny accents playing rock 'n' roll music. As long as the music's good. And our music's good, we've got funny haircuts and funny accents, it's all there, ain't it?"

Noel was dead on the money as usual. The thing that the U.S. liked about Oasis came down to the simplest factors: good tunes and a bad attitude. As their seventh tour of the States opened in Kansas City on February 23, the band found that the American audiences were starting to resemble the mad-for-it crowds back home.

"Oasis have gone to America six times in two years and that's how they've done it," Alan McGee explained in *NME*. "It's Noel's songs, Liam's voice, Liam's sex appeal, the right management and the right record label. They've got the lot."

Marcus Russell concurred. "Why have they done well in America? They're a great band, great songs, great live band, and they work hard. That adds up to success anywhere. I wouldn't say America is at their feet yet, but I'm excited. The hard work counts but you've got to have the material as well as being prepared to work."

"It's weird," Noel noted. "If you took a kid from the Bronx and a kid from Brixton who probably have absolutely nothing in common whatsoever, the one thing they'd have in common is they'd own a copy of *Morning Glory*."

"America's big and weird and fucking huge and it frightens the life out of me," the usually fearless Liam told *Raygun*. "It takes me time to get me head around it."

To be fair, a great many Americans were equally confused by Oasis. When one Yank fan told the bearded Liam that he resembled Charles Manson, the singer went ballistic.

"What are you talking about?" he snarled. "Have you ever seen Charlie Manson onstage singing with a band?"

The official proof of their U.S. breakout came when they got the proverbial picture on the cover of the *Rolling Stone*, though getting Liam and Noel's picture taken turned out to be a bit of a nightmare for the *RS* photographer.

"We turn up for the cover shoot," Noel said in *Select*, "me and Our Kid, right? And we go, 'Right, an hour, and then we're fucking leaving, we've got bad hangovers.' We only do half an hour for any other cunt in England, so it gets to an hour and this bloke's been fiddling about all afternoon. It suddenly dawned on me that he didn't know what the fuck he was doing.

"So I said to him, 'Have you ever done this before, you cunt, or what?' He says, 'No, no, I usually do fashion shoots. This is the first time I ever photographed a band.' So I said to the woman from *Rolling Stone*, 'Are you taking the fucking piss?' And she goes, 'Well, usually our cover shoots take about eight hours. When Pearl Jam did it . . . '

"We were like, 'You could not have picked one single worse fuckin' sentence in the world. You have got precisely another eight minutes to get this cover and we're out of here.' "

The antipathy between Oasis and America's big rock stars

was more than mutual. As they grew bigger and bigger in the States, Yank rockers began lashing out at their attitude, their arrogance, anything. In one of her infamous Internet diatribes, the First Lady of Alt Rock, Ms. Courtney Love-Cobain, pointed to the American rock community's fears: "Oasis must die. Do not buy Oasis records. They will come to rape and pillage our women and invade America."

Bearded Soundgarden axman Kim Thayil was unequivocal in his distaste for Oasis, telling *Melody Maker*, "I've only heard that one song, 'Wonderwall,' but I think it's crap! I saw it on MTV and it seemed to me to be kind of smarmy and contentless."

But he had to admit that he knew other musicians who thought that Oasis were swell indeed. "I was talking to Michael Stipe from R.E.M.," Thayil said, "and he was telling me how he thought they were fantastic live. He'd seen Oasis live and he thought they were interesting songwriters and very charismatic."

While the Gallaghers had nothing but contempt for their American peers, they were beginning to enjoy the country. At the very least, the trips to the States were almost like vacations from the increasing glare of the public eye. They didn't have to deal with the constant barrage of journalists and photographers and screaming fans following their every step. In America, they could put one hundred percent on the gigs themselves, because, to be honest, there wasn't much time to do anything else. "The worst thing about touring in America is that the distance between gigs is unreal, man," Noel told *Guitar Player*. "Driving for days, it's a pain in the arse."

Though he still enjoyed playing to U.S. crowds, there was one aspect of the American rock audience that baffled him to no end. "There's always someone in the front giving you the finger," Noel noted in wonderment. "Did they queue up for six hours just to come down and call me a wanker? I don't understand that mentality. It's very strange."

Liam also had mixed feeling about the States. "I like American birds," the studly one commented, "till they open their mouths. Then they annoy me. But if they're fit, they're fit." (This braggadocio came in spite of his ongoing relationship with "his dove," Patsy Kensit. Liam spent much of the U.S. journey telling anyone who'd listen that "I'm in love. . . . It's the best fuckin' feeling in the world. The biggest fuckin' high, know what I mean?")

On the other side of the coin, Americans never could get their heads around the Oasis obsession with the Fab Four, for some reason seeing the Gallaghers' passion as sacrilegious. The band were queried about it mercilessly. "There isn't a day that goes by that I don't listen to the Beatles," Noel explained to *Us* magazine's Jon Wiederhorn. "I'm obsessed with everything they've done, from their clothes to their music. I just stop short at going out with Japanese artists."

Liam defended his retro tastes in *Raygun*, telling Ken Micallef that "I'm twenty-two and I totally live in the past and I think it's top. All my mates are into the fucking Chemical Brothers. I hate it. Nonimaginative bollocks keyboard crap. If a new reggae band comes up, they don't get slated. No one says. 'You're retro.' It's just reggae music. But if you're doing rock 'n' roll, everyone says you're living in the past. Rock 'n' roll will never die. It will get done by other people, like me and Bonehead, but rock 'n' roll will never die."

As the tour rolled along, Noel was booked to perform an acoustic set at a big radio festival held in the New Jersey ski resort of Great Gorge. Though the lineup also featured Garbage and Stabbing Westward, the promotors dubbed the event "SnOasis" in honor of the biggest star on the bill. Unfortunately, a minor blizzard and freezing temperatures put the kibosh on Noel's performance, and he walked off after just two tunes. "He just physically couldn't move his fingers to play," said the Oasis spokesguy. "Everyone in the audience was in full-on ski gear, but you can't play in that. If you wear a thermal hat, you can't hear yourself, and if you wear gloves you can't play guitar."

After a much warmer gig at the Paramount Theater in New York City—a far cry from Wetlands—they returned home to London, where the Sex Pistols were coming together to announce that they had been lured by the big bucks to reunite. At the press conference held at the 100 Club, site of both the Pistols' and Oasis' early victories, Johnny Rotten was asked what he thought of Oasis. "They're just a pop band, you know," he replied, though Glen Matlock was mock anxious about commenting. "Don't wanna say anything about them," he trembled. "They're really hard and they might hit us."

But as the Pistols were reuniting, the Gallaghers announced that they were splitting up. Not Liam and Noel, mind, but the Irish cover band that had received Liam's seal of approval a few months back. Russell Nomark, manager of the now numero-uno tribute act, No Way Sis, was as cocky about his band's victory as a real Gallagher. "It's a sad day for the Irish folk scene," he sniffed.

In Dublin for a weekend of shows at the Point, Friday night's post-gig bash saw Liam and Patsy engaging in a major lovers' quarrel over Liam's flirting with Brit soap sexpot Anna Friel. Back in the privacy of their hotel suite at the Westbury Hotel, Patsy scooped up Liam's clothes and tossed them out the window while her furious sweetheart trashed the room. She flew back to London, and the Oasis spokesman told the dish-hungry press that he "didn't think Liam and Patsy were still a couple."

After the second night's show, the Gallaghers had a run-in with someone they liked even less than Damon Albarn. A *News of the World* reporter brought Liam and Noel's estranged father, Tommy, to the hotel where Oasis were staying. After somehow gaining access to his sons, who did not want to see him, an argument broke out. Reports of what happened next were blurry and biased. The tabloids claimed Liam and his old man wound up punching it out and had to be pulled apart, but the ever-present Oasis spokesperson denied those stories. "They were saying things, trying to goad Liam into reacting, but the boys kept their cool. Then the hotel security asked Tommy and the reporter to leave. Two police came, but they had been outside the hotel for most of the weekend dealing with the sheer volume of fans."

A round of European dates followed, and then they headed back to the U.S. once again, this time to cover the western half of the country. From the get-go, it looked to be a doomed trip. The first gig, at Vancouver B.C.'s Pacific Coliseum, turned ugly when the audience began flinging coins and such at the band. Noel warned the crowd that they would walk, though Liam couldn't resist taunting his antagonists. "Look, I'm here," he shouted from the edge of the stage. "Take your best shot."

Two songs later, a shoe landed at Liam's feet. True to their word, the band called it quits and walked off, with Liam telling the crowd that the band weren't "fucking monkeys," but, "the best band in the world!"

Meanwhile, one of Noel's gods, *Definitely Maybe* cover star Burt Bacharach, had told U.K. DJ Chris "Ginger Bollocks" Evans that he was planning to meet with Noel after Oasis' Los Angeles gig. "I do like him a lot," the songwriting legend said. "We talked on the phone three or four weeks ago. He was trying to get me and I was trying to get him back. And we got a date to get together and say hello. We'll probably meet in Santa Monica right after their concert."

Unfortunately, the Los Angeles show fell victim to the Oasis curse. Noel came down with a particularly vicious case of tonsilitis, the hard living catching up to him once again. Doctors advised him to take a few days off if he wanted to continue with the remainder of the tour, so shows in L.A. and Mesa, Arizona, were postponed.

They managed to play the final three dates on the trek, in Denver, Dallas, and Austin, but there was a bad vibe beginning to dog them in America. Considering the fact that every one of Oasis' U.S. tours had seen them failing to play one gig or another, your more paranoid Yank might have felt that the Gallaghers just didn't give a rat about their fans, that they really didn't matter all that much.

"It is important, obviously," Noel argued. " 'Cos we can't really go round saying we're the greatest band in the world if America doesn't know who the fuck we are. To be the greatest band in the world, you've gotta sell the most records and play the biggest gigs. But, having said that, we're not gonna be slaves to it, know what I mean? We're not gonna start kissing record-company arse. We've never done that and we never fuckin' will do. So it's like we come over on our own terms. The main reason we're here is 'cos of 'Wonderwall.' We delivered the goods and they fuckin' sold."

seventeen

feeling holy

They had survived another wearying trip to America, and now Manchester would show them how much they'd been missed. The two Maine Road shows, long sold out, beckoned.

Their homecoming was a mixed bag of triumphant return and superstar terror. After a string of death and kidnap threats, Liam and Noel were forced to hire a round-the-clock security force of almost a dozen guards. According to the Oasis spokesperson, the threats were being taken "very seriously," and they believed the harrassing phone calls and letters "might stem from rivalry between Manchester United and City. The band are all a bit paranoid and it's not being taken lightly. They are never out of the security staff's sight and nobody's taking any chances."

"Those guys who want to kidnap me had better hurry up and do a good job," Liam challenged, "because we'll all be waiting for them." As a result of the possibly hazardous conditions, the security squad kept the band members on the move so that their whereabouts would remain secret. They were booked into a series of Manchester hotels, canceling at the last minute, then finally ending at a cloistered, security-ringed country hotel about an hour from the stadium.

Outside the stadium, chaos reigned. Scalpers hawked the £17.50 tickets for a whopping £200. Tony McCarroll, who resided just yards from Maine Road, had to flee to the Lake District for the weekend.

Finally, showtime. As the punters on the terraces went berserk, Liam stepped out with an opening, "Are you mad for it, Manchester?" then warning the screaming crowd, "Don't have a piss in the stands, because I'll be standing there next week!"

Though the set was pretty much the standard Oasis live show, the energy, love, and passion the band felt from the enraptured audience pushed them to new heights of glory. They even felt compelled to do something they didn't do often: encores. As they left the stage, Noel bid a fond farewell "to the greatest fans in the world from the greatest band in the world."

Playing Maine Road meant a lot to the band. Liam explained after the first gig that "today was something else, just 'cos it was the place I used to come every Saturday, watch Big Joe Corrigan and the rest of it, and now it's us. It's like, yes, thank you."

Noel and Liam had reportedly made a bid to take over the Man City sponsorship from Brother Electronics for the sum of £650,000. This would have put the Oasis logo on the team's sky-blue uniform, but the busy Oasis spokesguy had to explain that while, yes, the Gallaghers had met with team executives, it was "not about sponsorship."

With all the hubbub, Noel was beginning to believe the hype. "The truth is," he told *Melody Maker*'s Ben Stud, "that to kids that are sixteen and that, we do mean a fuck of a lot. We are their Beatles.

"Because we were bigmouths when we started it," he continued, "we're gonna have to pull it off now! I don't actually know what 'the biggest band in the world' means. I just want to be as big as we can be and I don't want to leave any avenue unventured. We just want to do anything that's in our power and not have any regrets, never think, 'Oh, we should have done this or we should have done that.' "

The weekend was not trouble-free. There were reports of people being mugged and bottled by roaming gangs of kids. A security guard was knocked unconscious in a rush of fans seeking free entry to the stadium. The Manchester Police were criticized by the promotors, who called their lack of prescence "disgraceful."

"The police weren't involved in the licensing of the event," they explained, "so they took a decision between themselves not to be represented at the event and only act as a reactive force, not a deterrent."

No matter. The weekend was a clear-cut victory for Oasis. The official Maine Road program summed it up: "Hey now. It's about much more than words. Always has been, always will be. And anyone that doesn't realize that shouldn't be here. It's about something exhilarating, instinctive, inspirational. Something special: ROCK 'N' ROLL."

Soon after the triumphant Maine Road shows, Oasis announced their upcoming summer spectaculars. The 125,000 tickets for the August 10 show at Knebworth sold out within four hours. A second show was immediately announced and that, too, was sold out by the end of the business day, leading promoters MCP to dub the gigs "the fastest-selling concerts in the U.K., ever." Up in Scotland, tickets for two shows at Loch Lomond, at 40,000 each night, also blew out of the box office almost instantly.

A survey in the British trade mag, *Music Week*, found Oasis to be the U.K.'s favorite band by an "overwhelming majority." "This survey puts Oasis up there as a classic band alongside the greats like the Beatles, the Rolling Stones, Led Zeppelin, and Bob Marley," the Oasis spokesguy boasted in an official statement, though they humbly added, "Are they bigger than the Beatles? That's blasphemy!"

The band had gone from playing dank pubs to gigantic fields in less than two years, and Noel had to figure out how to create a similar vibe in a very different venue. "Well, a football-fucking-ground is a football ground and they're pretty impersonal," he said to *NME*'s Andy Richardson. "We're trying to look at venues that have a bit of character, like Loch Lomond, obviously Maine Road just for the vibe because we're all City supporters. . . . We want to do stuff that hasn't been done before, or stuff that hasn't been done for years and years. We're just trying to keep it interesting for us.

"It's weird that we're having to move outdoors," he went on. "I suppose it comes with being a big fuck-off dirty great big horrible rock band. You have to move outdoors unless you play to an elitist audience and we've never been about that in the first place."

With the media demonizing the band at every opportunity, the residents of Balloch, Scotland—the site of the upcoming Loch Lomond gigs—began to worry. "Balloch is a lovely little postcard village where the more mature person comes to relax," council member Margaret McGregor said. "All we need is nearly 100,000 people fired up on booze and everything else to come rampaging through here."

As Oasis became more and more successful, Oasis wannabes began sprouting up all over England. Classicist combos like Ocean Colour Scene and Cast were dubbed "Noelrock." In a show of support, Noel and Liam turned up two nights in a row for Ocean Colour Scene at the London Electric Ballroom. On the second night, they performed a short surprise set featuring unplugged versions of "Wonderwall," "Cast No Shadow," and "Live Forever," in addition to joining OCS for an encore rendition of "Day Tripper."

Their old pal Tony Griffiths of the Real People was in attendance that night. "We didn't know they were coming," he said after, "but it was pretty impressive. . . . The crowd couldn't really believe it."

The problem was, most of the Noelrockers—Northern Uproar, Smaller, and so forth—were simply not as inspired, interesting, or just plain talented as the band that had bestowed blessing upon them. "It's not their fault that all the bands that followed in their wake, with or without their seal of approval, have been unspeakably shite," said the Boo Radleys' Martin Carr. "It's not their fault that they don't fit into people's ideas of rock stars who should be saving whales and rescuing cats from trees. How refreshing it is to have a band that big and realize they don't have to be steamin' wanksocks like Sting."

That month saw Noel awarded the Ivor Novello Songwriter of the Year trophy by the British Academy of Songwriters and Authors, but when he heard that he was to split the prize with Damon Albarn, he regretfully declined, calling the joint award a "cheap publicity stunt."

With their new superstar status, Noel and Meg were flown to the Cannes Film Festival for the premiere of *Trainspotting*, the film that, with its energetic rock 'n' roll heart and frenzied drug use, could rightly be called the Oasis of the cinema. The fact that Noel was even invited to this prestigious event was a reflection of just how big Oasis had become.

"Two years ago I wouldn't have been asked to the Cannes Film Festival," he told *Select*. "Fine, arsed. Now, of course, after 'Wonderwall' and 'Don't Look Back in Anger,' they draw up their celebrity wish list and I'm on it . . . Now all these people wanna meet me, see. Al Pacino, Mick Jagger . . . Their PR'll go, 'See that geezer over there, that's the bloke from Oasis, it'd be cool if you all were over there and you had your picture taken.' "

Also in attendance were rock royalty like Elton John and, much to Noel's chagrin, Damon Albarn and Justine Frischmann. "When I got back," Noel said, "I read a piece and he said, 'I went to Cannes and Noel Gallagher followed me around everywhere. . . . ' Like I've got fuck-all better to do than get on a plane to Cannes to follow you around with your fucking ugly bird!"

While he found *Trainspotting* to be "top," Noel told Chris Evans that the best film at Cannes was a new version of Hans Christian Anderson's children's classic, *Thumbelina*. "We haven't actually seen it yet," he chuckled, "but on the billboards it says, '*Thumbelina*: Three birds, three pairs of knickers, and a great film.' We haven't seen it, but I'm telling you now, we're there!"

Back home, Liam had a far friendlier encounter with Damon

when he led a Noel-less Oasis in a charity soccer match at London's Mile End Stadium, with the proceeds going to the Nordoff-Robbins Music Therapy for disabled children. The afternoon's high point was the moment when the giddy Liam went up to his foe and yanked down his pants, exposing Albarn's bum to the screams of the crowd. Despite this psych-out, the Blur squad came out the winner, beating Liam and the lads 2–0.

In June, Noel finally hooked up with his great hero, songwriter Burt Bacharach, a moment that he described to *Select* as "quite ludicrous."

"He's sixty-seven and I'm twenty-nine," he explained. "Could be my granddad. I mean, what do you talk to him about? I was just coming on like, 'D'ya like the Clash?' He's like, 'Uh, I can't say I've ever heard of them.' Then he idles over to the piano on the other side of the room and starts playing the intro to "This Guy's in Love with You." Then he turns around to me and goes, 'Just join in, man.' I'm sat there thinking, 'How the fuck did I get here?' "

It got even weirder when Noel joined Burt onstage at the London Royal Festival Hall to sing the aforementioned Bacharach-David hit. Meg, Liam, and Patsy were all in the audience to show their support, as were Gallagher pals Kate Moss and Johnny Depp.

"It was the most nerve-racking thing I've ever done," Noel said afterwards. "I've never been onstage to sing without a guitar before and I didn't know what to do. I kept looking for Our Kid to come on and bail me out."

July passed relatively quietly, as the band prepared for the big August weekenders. Speaking to Radio One DJ Jo Whiley, Noel revealed that he had written and demoed thirteen complete songs for a new album while away on holiday with Meg. "It's a great album," he said, getting ahead of himself a tad, "a bit of a mix between *Definitely Maybe* and *(What's the Story?)*. I've played the songs to the band and they're all pretty chuffed."

More proof of their unstoppable rise came when it was revealed that Liam and Noel had officially joined the ranks of the superfamous with their inclusion in the 1996 edition of *The International Who's Who*. Editor Richard Fitzwilliams explained that "it's very important for books of this sort to keep up-to-date with current trends. And Oasis are currently so successful, we're thinking of putting the whole band in next year's issue, something we haven't done since the Beatles."

Meanwhile, the legal battle between Oasis and Tony McCarroll was postponed until the end of 1997. A High Court judge was told that a deal had been struck between McCarroll and the other members of Oasis over royalties claimed by the ex-drummer. After a brief hearing, McCarroll's attorney told the presiding judge that the band had agreed to pay him 80 percent of his one-fifth share of royalties from *Definitely Maybe*, as well as "Whatever" and "Some Might Say."

August arrived and it was time to play Loch Lomond. Despite the accidental death of a site crew worker the evening before, the weekend, though racked with miserable weather, was fraught with positive vibrations.

Liam greeted the Loch Lomond throng with his usual charm. "We've been away for three months," he shouted, "pickin' our noses and scratchin' our bottoms and it's good to see youse all 'avin' it!"

The singer was in fine form, carrying his tambourine around in his mouth while not singing, and barking madness at the audience and the band. Liam had little patience with the long feedback-laced Noel solos that seemed to end every tune. "I know yer good," he groused at one point, "but end the fuckin' song, alright? I wanna find out what the next song is."

A number of fans climbed up the sound towers to catch a better view, though they ended up distracting the lead singer. "Get off the fuckin' scaffolding," Liam scolded. "Like, it's confusing me. I'm singing 'Supersonic' and I'm thinking, 'Get off the scaffolding!' It's like, I don't know the lyrics as it is!"

For "Live Forever," the giant video screens displayed a roll call of dead rockers—John Lennon, Jimi Hendrix, Kurt Cobain—while a string and brass section were brought out for a hanful of tunes including a sterling "The Masterplan."

The following weekend the Oasis juggernaut hit Knebworth. The show was essentially the same as Loch Lomond, only much, much bigger. The guest list alone numbered 7,000! The vast field of fans was enthralled by the Oasis spectacular, singing along to every song, with the possible exception of the two new tunes making their debut: the punky "My Big Mouth" and "It's Getting Better, Man."

For the encore, John Squire made his first post–Stone Roses appearance, adding soaring axework to "Champagne Supernova" and the closing "I Am the Walrus." Fireworks bloomed in the sky, just as they emerged from the enormous PA.

Before the second night's show, Noel considered the mind-blowing experience of playing to such a huge crowd. "I've been trying to put it into words," he told *Select*'s Andrew Perry, "and I'd rather not fucking try, to tell you the truth. There's big, then there's bigger than big and then there's fuckin' like last night. . . . Now that is big.

"You can't ask for advice off anyone who's been there before," he noted, "because no one has. Apart from Dave Gilmour and that. You know, I've got a few things to say to Phil Collins, but asking for advice wouldn't be fucking one of them. . . ."

eighteen

serve the servants

And then everything went to hell.

The masterplan had reached the moment of recording the long-anticipated *MTV Unplugged*. The event was kept top-secret, with only a select four hundred contest winners in attendance at London's Royal Festival Hall.

But those fortunate few were in for a disappointment. Liam decided that he was not going to be joining the band for the performance, pleading vocal troubles. According to the omnipresent spokesman, the singer had already received hospital treatment for laryngitis at a King's Cross hospital.

As Liam, Patsy, and Meg sat in a private box above, Noel informed the audience that "Liam's got a sore throat and he can't sing, but you've still got the four of us." Actually there were quite a bit more that just the four Oasis lads onstage. They were accompanied by a piano player, an organist, and a harmonica player, as well as the string and brass sections that had joined them at Loch Lomond and Knebworth.

Despite his—ahem—sore throat, Liam spent the gig smoking and chugging lager, occasionally barking abuse and throwing two fingers at his brother, who carried on nonetheless.

It wasn't just the fans who were heartbroken by the lead singer's disappearing act. An MTV spokesman told the press that they were "very disappointed," and that the video network had yet to make a decision on whether or not the show would air.

Creation spokesguy Johnny Hopkins made the official not-that-big-a-deal, postshow statement. "Liam has had a problem with his throat and regretfully had to sit the gig out," Hopkins said. "Noel, the Chief, took charge of the vocals. Liam was disappointed not to be able to perform for his fans, but he got a rare opportunity to see how brilliant Oasis are live."

Just days later, Liam announced that he would also be sitting out the upcoming U.S. tour. He decided not to board a Chicago-bound plane at London's Heathrow Airport with the rest of Oasis, literally minutes before takeoff.

Later that day, as a horde of tabloid press decended upon the home he shared in the plush St. John's Wood district of London with Patsy and her son, Liam explained that his reason for bagging the trip was so that he and his honey could go house-hunting.

"The house has just been sold and I'm having moving problems," he told reporters. "We have go to be out by the weekend. I am not going around touring in the U.S. when I've got nowhere to live."

Though he intended to fly over at some point, he figured that the rest of the group would get on just fine with Noel taking the mike. "The band are going to try to do it without me," Liam said. "If they can't do it, I guess I'll go back. I don't care about the tour. I am sick of living my life in hotels. I need to be happy. I've got to find a place to live."

The pressure of being in Oasis had finally gotten to Liam. The tabs went nuts over the story. Headlines blared "What's the Story? Liam Quits the Tour-y" and "Patsy's Got Him by the Wonderballs." The possibility of England's favorite sons' imminent collapse was a huge story, with Kensit being branded as the Yoko of Oasis. A rare Oasis silence went into effect with the only comments coming from Liam, who occasionally poked his head out to give two fingers to the press, sometimes informing them of the rugby scores. Though a few American ticketholders asked for refunds when Liam failed to show, most fans either didn't care or just came to see the freak show. A wan Noel handled the vocal duties at the tour's opening gig in Chicago, and from all accounts the set was not among their best. Noel and the band were plainly tired, stressed out, and none too thrilled at returning to smaller venues after the triumphs of the summer.

Liam finally relented and flew to Chicago to meet up with the rest of the band for the next night's show in Detroit. Upon his arrival he was met by the now ever-present mob of journos and paparazzi. Gallagher answered questions with a stream of swearing, and said his priority was himself and not his fans or anyone else.

Liam took the stage that Friday night a three-quarters-full Palace of Auburn Hills in suburban Detroit and made no acknowledgment of the week's events, simply letting the lyrics to "Hello" do the talking: "It's good to be back," he sang, though he probably didn't mean it.

Along for the ride were two of their labelmates, Manic Street Preachers (who, having supported Oasis at Maine Road and Knebworth, were used to the madness) as well as the Seattle post-grunge combo Screaming Trees, whose lead singer Mark Lanegan had recently gone off about Oasis in the press. "They're a bunch of big-mouthed pussies!" Lanegan challenged in *Melody Maker*. "Anybody who's got to talk that much about how bad-assed they are is just a fuckin' pussy in my book. A real man doesn't have to talk about it, does he? Maybe I'll run into them in a dark alley some time and we'll find out who the real man is."

Well, through the synergistic magic of the record industry, Lanegan got his wish. Though Liam and Lanegan never came to blows backstage, the garrulous Gallagher kept getting into the Seattle sad sack's face, feigning an inability to recall his support band's moniker. "Barking Branches?" he poked. "Crazy Conkers?"

The tour hit New York for a pair of gigs at the Jones Beach

Amphitheater on Long Island, as well as an appearance at the annual MTV Music Video Awards. Here was a chance to show all of America—and the world—just how brilliant Oasis were in performance.

Asked who else he was looking forward to seeing on the awards show, Liam was his arrogant self. "None," he said. "They're all shit. Fugees? Crap. Oasis. That's it."

Liam was psyched-up for the appearance, though his brother was getting a little worn out by the powder keg–like atmosphere. Before the awards Noel, Liam, and Guigsy were cornered by MTV's John Norris as they walked from their hotel to Radio City. Noel busted his chops about how their last interview was subtitled for the Americans. "I think we were speaking quite loud and clear, actually."

A flustered Norris got off a few more questions to minimal response, when Noel turned the tables on him, whipping out a microphone of his own. "So tell me," he asked the stunned VJ for no apparent reason, "what's it like being a transvestite?"

Utterly confused, Norris tried his luck with Guigsy, asking if he was looking forward to the awards. Guigsy cut him off with a curt, "No, not at all."

Noel continued taking the piss, cracking wise about his pal Lars Ulrich of Metallica, and generally making Norris squirm. The reporter finally asked Liam what the differences between the American and British audiences were. "They're all the same, aren't they," said Liam. "They're all here for one reason, to see the greatest rock 'n' roll band in the world. They all clap, they all shout."

The band was not nominated for a single prize, though they were clearly one of the evening's most anticipated moments. The Smashing Pumpkins were shaping up to be the night's big winners, and the show had featured songs from a number of megastars, from LL Cool J to Neil Young. Then came magic time.

"After this break . . . most or all of Oasis, live!!"

Oasis were introduced—via satellite—by *Trainspotting* stars Ewan MacGregor and Ewan Bremner. Between the seven-second delay and his Manchester drawl, Liam's pronouncement to the star-studded crowd—not to mention the 300 million viewers worldwide—

was near unintelligible. "I hope you're having a good time," he slurred, "but I know you're having a shit time. You're all bored and too scared to admit it."

They kicked into a full-steam-ahead "Champagne Supernova," the long-tressed Liam deliciously bored and angry, his voice the perfect weapon. He was in a piss-taking mood, changing the lyric to "a champagne supernova up your bum," as Noel looked on, exasperated. He paced during Noel's ferocious solo, standing center stage for a moment to dangle a huge saliva gob at his feet. He threw his beer at the audience, showed them his rear, Jarvis style, and walked off.

Some in the crowd just didn't get it. Host Dennis Miller, for one, was unamused. "Wow," he said as Oasis walked off, "he spilt a beer!"

On the other hand, their fellow musicians were impressed. "I thought it was cool," said slacker king Beck, "We were all digging it. We like spit."

"They rocked!" exclaimed Billy Corgan backstage.

But all was not rockin' with Oasis. After their performance, the band simply skipped out, avoiding any after-parties or press conferences. There was plainly tension in the air. The Brothers Gallagher were just not getting along.

The Long Island shows went off as planned, but as the tour bus ventured south, things began to get ugly. The post-Knebworth pressure, the poor U.S. ticket sales, the tabloid assaults on Liam and Patsy, the strain of being on the road for nearly three years, all finally caught up to Oasis. Just as the band had grown bigger and bigger, this time the inevitable explosion would be positively nuclear.

The bomb finally dropped in North Carolina. The venue for their September 12 show in Charlotte had been changed from the 12,000-seat Independence Arena to the far-smaller, 2,500-capacity Hornet Training Facility, and Noel was fed up. He had simply had enough. Just two hours before they were to play, he informed the band that he was going home.

Red-eyed and blue, Noel grabbed the next plane to London

out of Atlanta, with the band following suit the next day. Neither Noel nor Liam, both usually fond of flinging insults at the ever-present crowd of press, said a word to the swarm of journalists and photographers that met them at the airport. The word on the street was that Oasis were kaput. The *Sun* ran with the mindblowing headline, "BLOWASIS!" and the stories of fistfights and cold shoulders soon emerged. Apparently the feuding brothers had had to be separated as they exchanged blows after a five-hour emergency "summit meeting" in their Charlotte hotel. It was said that Liam had made a number of teary calls to his mam, complaining about the tour and Noel. The Oasis spokesperson wouldn't confirm anything, only saying that yes, there were "internal differences," yes, the U.S. tour was canceled, and no, he didn't know if the band had indeed split up.

"The future of Oasis is unknown," Creation's Johnny Hopkins told the *Sun*. "It is open-ended. It is too early to say if the split is permanent. We just don't know."

As the British papers screamed, a nation wept. A stream of damage-control press statements sprang forth from the Oasis camp. First it was announced that the band would cease from touring in the "foreseeable future," forcing the cancellation of a European tour and the first Oasis assault on Australia. However, the spokesperson stressed, "in every other aspect Oasis will continue to exist and function as a band."

Liam and Noel were said to be together at an undisclosed location, getting over jet lag and trying to figure out what to do. Though a press conference was slated, in the end, the brothers decided to let the spokesman do the talking The press release explained that Oasis were fine, and since they'd arrived home early, they could now begin working on their third album. Most importantly, the band wanted everyone to know that the troubles were not the result of any outside elements, i.e., Patsy, poor ticket sales, et cetera.

"It was a decision taken solely by Noel Gallagher on behalf of his four friends," the statement read. "We look forward to presenting our fans with a new album in the summer of '97. It ain't over till it's over. Keep the faith."

not fade away

"We never should have gone to America then," Liam told *The Face*. "We should have had time off after Knebworth. The band didn't fall out; it was just that we got sick of the touring. We'd been on a bus for the last two or three years and we just woke up. . . . We were in a hotel near Atlanta and Noel came down one morning and said he was going home. We all wanted to go home before, and I was like, 'Fucking top one, man! It's been ages! When's the flight?' "

After the dust settled, Oasis got back to business. Noel rediscovered his roots in dance music, first collaborating with the Chemical Brothers on the banging technopop "Setting Sons"—which, in the heat of October's Oasismania, entered the U.K. chart at number one—and then remixed a track from Beck's *Odelay!* LP. Funnily enough, Noel removed much of the hip-hoppiness from the tune "Devil's Haircut" and rocked it up, accentuating the guitars and drums. He sang the praises of sample-king DJ Shadow and even threatened to release his long-hidden late-eighties house tracks.

Liam, on the other hand, returned to the difficult job of being Liam. He engaged in a number of public spats with his dove,

Patsy, got busted for cocaine possession (though he escaped charges with a caution from police), flicked a cigarette ash on Mick Jagger's head, and generally continued to make a fool out of himself as only he could.

Most importantly, Oasis entered Abbey Road Studios—the site of the Beatles' most inventive work—to record their next record, yogically titled *Be Here Now*. Liam described the record's first single, "It's Getting Better, Man," to *The Face* as "rawer ... a bit 'Street Fighting Man,' with maracas." As is his wont, Noel promised a blend of *Definitely Maybe* with *Morning Glory*, guaranteeing a handful of number ones to come.

With 20 million records sold worldwide, Oasis—Liam, Noel, Bonehead, Guigsy, and Whitey—lived up to the goals they had set right from the start. Their dreams of world domination had come true, and no matter what disasters had befallen them on their journey from Manchester to the tippy-top, they had somehow managed to stay together to fight another day.

Bonehead was philosophical about the future: "I know for a fact that when this ends I'll walk round the corner to my local pub and he'll be sitting there. And I'll say, 'Liam, let's get a beer.' And we'll get fuckin' lushed up."

"We are the biggest band in Britain of all time, ever," Noel crowed in *Select*. "The funny thing is, that fucking mouthing-off three years ago about how we were gonna be the biggest band in the world, we actually went and done it. And it was a piece of piss."

discography

U.K. Singles

Supersonic (CRESCD176)
Supersonic
Take Me Away
I Will Believe (live)
Columbia (white-label demo)

Shakermaker (CRESCD182)
Shakermaker
D'Yer Wanna Be a Spaceman?
Alive (8-track demo)
Bring It On Down (live)

Live Forever (CRESCD185)
Live Forever
Up In the Sky (acoustic)
Cloudburst
Supersonic (live)

Cigarettes & Alcohol (CRESCD190)
Cigarettes & Alcohol
I Am the Walrus (live)
Listen Up
Fade Away

Whatever (CRESCD195)
Whatever
(It's Good) to Be Free
Half the World Away
Slide Away

discography

Some Might Say (CRESCD204)
Some Might Say
Talk Tonight
Acquiesce
Headshrinker

Roll With It (CRECD212)
Roll With It
It's Better People
Rockin' Chair
Live Forever (live)

Wonderwall (CRECD215)
Wonderwall
Round Are Way
The Swamp Song
The Masterplan

Don't Look Back In Anger (CRECD221)
Don't Look Back In Anger
Step Out
Underneath the Sky
Cum On Feel the Noize

U.K. Singles Box Sets

Definitely Maybe Singles Box (CREDM001)
includes:
Supersonic
Shakermaker
Live Forever
Cigarettes & Alcohol
Oasis Interviews (CCV001)

(What's the Story) Morning Glory? Singles Box (CREMG001)
includes:
Some Might Say
Roll With It
Wonderwall
Don't Look Back In Anger
Oasis Interviews (CCV001)

U.S. Singles

Wonderwall (49K 78204)
Wonderwall
Round Are Way
Talk Tonight
Rockin' Chair
I Am the Walrus (live)

Albums

Definitely Maybe (CRE169/EK66431)
Rock 'n' Roll Star
Shakermaker
Live Forever
Up In the Sky
Columbia
Supersonic
Bring It On Down
Cigarettes & Alcohol
Digsy's Dinner
Slide Away
Married With Children

discography

(What's the Story) Morning Glory? (CRE189/EK67351)
Hello
Roll With It
Wonderwall
Don't Look Back In Anger
Hey Now!
Some Might Say
Cast No Shadow
She's Electric
Morning Glory
Champagne Supernova

acknowledgments

First off, I'd like to express undying gratitude to the folks of the much-maligned U.K. music press: *Melody Maker, NME, Select, Vox, Q,* and so forth. They are a constant influence on my writing and my listening. You've just got to learn how to read them. Special mention to the scribes who have had the inside skinny on Oasis since Day One: Paul Mathur, Jim Shelley, Ted Kessler, Simon Williams, Keith Cameron, Andy Richardson, and so many others. In a very real way, their documentation of the Oasis saga shows them to be as important to this story as Liam and Noel. Well, maybe Guigsy.

Without the support (on oh-so-many levels) of the following, the preceding would have been impossible: Deb Bernardini and Alan Brown, Leslie Bleakley, Randy Bookasta, Scott Booker, Tim Broun, Camilla Calthrop, the Family Cope, Ron Decker, Felice Ecker, Bobbie Gale, Rick Gershon, Matt Hendrickson, Mindy Labernz, John Loscalzo, Keith Lyle, Jackie Marlowe, Ken Micallef, Barbara Mitchell, Laura Morgan, Kurt B. Reighley, Ira Robbins, Lisa Ross, Paul Samuels, Seb Shelton, Dev Sherlock, Caffy St. Luce, Jill Tomlinson, Cat Tyc, Rick Vestuto, Amy Welch, Meryl Wheeler, Jon Wiederhorn, Luann Williams, Marcia Zellers, and C. J. Kitsos at Rudge Management, who scored me tickets for Knebworth.

Kudos to my fine attorney, Celeste Phillips.

Bonus kudos to Brian "The Brain" Berger who proved himself to be more than just mad... he's mad for it!

Bigtime gracias to Superagent Dave Dunton (not to mention his missus, Regina Joskow Dunton), as well as to the good folks in the Main Office: Jim Fitzgerald, Regan Good, Tara Schimming, and Dana Albarella.

A hug and a kiss to my mam, my pop, and my sister, who put up with a lot and never ask for anything in return.

acknowledgments

Special thanks to the Master himself, Martin Huxley, for his sage advice, encouragement, and sympathy.

Finally, I want to send love and "Live Forever" to the rest of the band. Without you guys, I'm nothing: Jason Cohen, Michelle Ferguson, Mike Flaherty, Jonathan Gordon, Robert Gottstein, Paul Kopasz, Robb Moore, Scott Schinder, and Ken Weinstein.